What is a LeaderShift?

Every once in a while in the course of history, a LeaderShift occurs. It usually comes unexpectedly, and it transforms the world for at least a generation. Past LeaderShifts include:

- The historical switch from kings and chiefs to community fathers such as doctors, lawyers, and town merchants
- The 1880s–1920s transition from city fathers to titans of industry, like Carnegie, Morgan, and Rockefeller
- The 1940s–1970s shift from business tycoons to managers, spurred by the work of Edward Deming and innovators from Jack Welch to Sam Walton
- The 1980s–1990s transition from managers to leaders, influenced by sages like Buckminster Fuller, Earl Nightingale, and Stephen Covey

Today, we are in the early stages of another great transition. Is your family, business, or nation prepared for the coming LeaderShift?

LeaderShift

A Call for Americans to Finally Stand Up and Lead

*Why We Need to Recognize and
Overcome the Five Laws of Decline*

———————

ORRIN WOODWARD
AND OLIVER DeMILLE

**BUSINESS
PLUS**

NEW YORK   BOSTON

Business Plus
Hachette Book Group
237 Park Avenue
New York, NY 10017

www.HachetteBookGroup.com

Printed in the United States of America

RRD-C

First Edition: April 2013
10 9 8 7 6 5 4 3 2

Business Plus is an imprint of Grand Central Publishing.
The Business Plus name and logo are trademarks of Hachette Book Group, Inc.

The Hachette Speakers Bureau provides a wide range of authors for speaking events. To find out more, go to www.hachettespeakersbureau.com or call (866) 376-6591.

The publisher is not responsible for websites (or their content) that are not owned by the publisher.

LCCN: 2013931787
ISBN 978-1-4555-7337-0

From Orrin: To my wife for her unyielding belief; to many leaders for their courageous words; and to freedom fighters throughout history for their sacrifice. I am inspired by your examples.

From Oliver: To James, George, Thomas, and John. Better friends and mentors are beyond my capacity to imagine.

Acknowledgments

What happens when a top leadership consultant who loves education (Orrin) combines with a great educator who has spent his career promoting leadership (Oliver) to write a book? The synergy of minds as we worked together on this project was magical. We were both surprised and moved by the results. We truly loved working together! Add to this mix our editor and friend Rick Wolff's impressive ability to turn good to great, and The LeaderShift was created. Indeed, Rick's comments, suggestions, and encouragement inspired us, and took the book to the next level.

We would like to thank our families, friends, business associates, and the many students who, over the years, have asked the tough questions that sharpened our thinking.

Special recognition to mastermind members Tim Marks, Claude Hamilton, George Guzzardo, Bill Lewis, and Dan Hawkins. Your drive for excellence in all areas is contagious!

Thanks to Laurie Woodward and Rachel DeMille (who read every version of the manuscript and provided numerous invaluable suggestions), Chris Brady and Stephen Palmer (who always urged us to turn a story on its head), and research assistant Sara DeMille (who endured the insane hours of a night-owl writer, helped put the polish on the end product, and was never afraid to argue a point when it really counted).

Oliver gives a special note of thanks to W. Cleon Skousen, his beloved mentor, and one of the earliest watchmen to see what was being lost and how to reclaim it. He believed unswervingly in the capability of regular men and women to govern themselves and the nation with wisdom and virtue.

Furthermore, special appreciation goes to the team at Business Plus, especially Meredith Haggerty and Carolyn Kurek. Their professionalism and expertise helped improve the book in so many ways, and they made the entire process enjoyable.

Lastly, we would like to thank our Lord and Savior Jesus Christ for His amazing grace and love.

Great men are they who see...that thoughts rule the world.

—RALPH WALDO EMERSON

LeaderShift

PART I

1

"Still watching, Mr. President. Nothing this year so far."

"Or this decade," the small man replied.

"Or even the last four decades," he muttered, as he turned and walked down the long hallway. His shoulders were slumped in what looked like disappointment. But those who knew him well understood that his feelings were a lot closer to despair.

Goodnight, David," Marcus said.

"I'll call tomorrow afternoon." David waved, as Marcus checked his watch and walked toward his BMW.

David smiled. Marcus checked his watch a lot whenever he had a new one and wanted to be sure everyone admired it. This time it was a new Tag Heuer Grand Carrera with the leisure racing band, and Marcus had mentioned in passing that it only cost him $10K. Last weekend it had been a Vacheron Constantin. David shook his head.

That's just the world we live in, sad as it is. Whoever has the most toys wins, and all that . . .

He turned and walked along the water of his private estate. The old feeling of frustration immediately came back as the lights from Marcus's car left the driveway and turned onto the main road. David had enjoyed the lighter mood during dinner with Marcus, but now the old worry returned.

I used to think that way, too.

David switched on his iPhone and glanced at the news updates. Arguments in Washington about tax increases. New regulations. Partisan battles. Fuel prices. He put the phone back into the safety of his pocket and kept walking.

I'd rather have Marcus's interest in shopping than the national addiction to bigger government. Thinking of these two things in the same sentence made him smile. *Together, these two views just about sum up today's America.* He sighed.

When he reached the end of the dock, he stopped and leaned on the rail. The lights from the city across the bay reflected off the water. It was beautiful, and David forced himself to listen to the waves against the dock and feel the breeze rather than think about...the thing.

David Mersher had been the CEO of Indytech for almost two decades, and the company he had founded was now a leading growth firm despite the struggling national and world economy. He had won more awards than he cared to remember, and his family was the joy of his life. His wife, Amy, had been his business partner from the beginning, and with his oldest daughter, Emily, finishing grad school this spring, many of his friends were suggesting that he relax more and enjoy the fruits of his success. "You've earned it," they told him. "Let others worry about the direction of the nation. It's not your problem."

He took a deep breath of ocean air. *I need to face this thing head-on. It's time to deal with it. It's festered too long.*

I know how to deal with these things, just like I always have. Directly and immediately.

David squared his shoulders and confronted the challenge he'd been feeling for months.

America is my homeland. I've been blessed with a wonderful wife and four hardworking children. Professionally, my life has been a blast, owning my own company and specializing in corporate turnarounds. I should be able to just relax and enjoy life.

But America's story is not inspiring. Well, not right now, anyway. It is bankrupting itself—interest on the national debt is one of America's greatest expenses, the welfare state has bred generational poverty and a widespread loss of self-respect, our national credit rating will most likely keep getting downgraded, and the international warring factions have turned our military into the world's largest police force.

With each passing election, many Americans think their vote has created some change, but the simple truth is—things keep heading in the wrong direction no matter who is in office.

Although I have been blessed personally with a beautiful family and a thriving business, what will that matter if freedom disappears from neglect? What kind of country will my children and grandchildren live in if leaders don't begin to arise in our generation—as they did in the founding era?

This is my problem. It is. In fact, this is everyone's problem. It's the biggest problem of our lives, and the more successful we've been, the more our leadership is needed. We don't need more watches or cars, or more taxes and regulations. We need leaders.

We need a nation of citizens who are leaders.

David's thoughts turned more personal. *For whatever reason, God has blessed me with the ability to identify the underlying systems of decline in corporations and then the ability to initiate a turnaround by redesigning the flawed systems. I've made millions doing just that.*

I know the answer. Since America is my home, I know I have to get involved in its turnaround. I spent the first half of my life achieving success in the corporate sector, so why not spend the second half influencing the public sector to ensure the same opportunities for future generations?

So many of my colleagues are building homes in other nations: New Zealand, Monaco, Costa Rica. They see the same problems in America, and yet they use their money and leadership to get away. Permanent vacations, I guess.

Now that he had taken on this project, David applied the same intense focus that had made him so adept at seeing through business failures over the years and understanding what was needed to turn a company around.

It usually only took a few key changes, and then relentless execution in following through. And that always meant the right kind of leadership.

What are the key changes needed in America?

David began to analyze with his trained expertise. For him, this was a discipline, an art and a science all rolled into one.

First, America's original foundational principles are in various states of disrepair through ignorance and neglect. They must be relearned and rebuilt.

David drew a deep breath.

This certainly won't be easy. In fact, even though I have had plenty of tough assignments in my life, this will be my biggest undertaking by far.

With so many Americans looking to the government as a nanny to take care of them, liberty is on its last legs. Running against the current is never an easy task, but when it's necessary, leaders must do it. Like one of my first mentors used to say: when the going gets tough, the tough get going. America is in a tough spot, and the tough need to get going.

David reflected on what he called the Five Laws of Decline (FLD). He had seen these in action in his work with a number of corporate clients.

Similar to how gravity must constantly be overcome in order for a plane to fly, each entity must overcome its own FLD to grow. In truth, it's not too much to say that this systematic approach to analyzing corporations is what has catapulted me to the top among turnaround specialists.

While it used to take me months to identify the root causes of a company's decline, now this can be accomplished in just a few weeks or less, simply because these principles are based upon human nature—human nature that hasn't changed at all in recorded history.

Now, apply these same principles to the nation. History is full of examples of empires that violated the FLD and fell over time. Greece,

Rome, and the British Empire are three applicable case studies. Thankfully, one doesn't have to read the thousands of history books, economics books, and political tracts to capture the essence of the FLD. The United States today is experiencing all Five Laws of Decline. It's time to figure out what is needed for effective turnaround.

David stopped to reflect. *Okay, time to let in the emotion. My walk this evening has filled me with a sense of responsibility to apply the FLD to our own country before it's too late. Actually, I've been feeling this way for a long time. But whom should I talk to? My consulting work has kept me too busy to develop a bunch of relationships in the political camps.*

Will my information even be welcome? Probably not. Most turnarounds fight the truth at first. The last thing I want to do is be a modern-day Cassandra—Homer's young lady of Troy who was cursed by the gods to speak the truth and yet be ignored as their city fell. Or Virgil, who warned of Rome's decline but whose words fell on deaf ears until it was too late.

That's the big one, David thought to himself. *What if it's too late? Okay, enough emotion.*

Despite my fears, I feel compelled to act.

2

"Mr. President, we ... may ... have ... found someone."

James sat up in bed. "Come in, young man. Tell me about it."

"I'm sorry I woke you, Mr. President, but you told me—"

"None of that, none of that," James cut him off. "Who is he? Or she? Which continent? How well prepared? Come on, man, speak!"

I t was too early to call for breakfast, or even to risk waking up Amy by rattling around in the kitchen. But David was absolutely starving.

He glanced at the clock behind him, though he knew perfectly well his laptop would tell him the time if he just looked down at the corner. He liked the big clock over the mantel, however, right above the framed pictures. His favorite was the famous photo of Vince Lombardi. Anyway, his habit was to use the big clock to check the time, and he wasn't going to go all digital now.

Five fifteen a.m. Still too early. I've been writing since two. This should be a good writing day, Marcus isn't expecting to hear from me until two or three this afternoon. David dismissed his growling stomach and turned back to his screen and keyboard.

He reviewed the PowerPoint he'd used hundreds of times to teach the Five Laws of Decline. His main point to his corporate clients: *ignore any one of these laws, and your company will start its decline.*

As he pulled up each slide, he reread the outline of his customary FLD speech:

> The first law of decline knocks leaders out of the "coma of complacency." In our egalitarian times, we like to feel that everyone is equal and that there isn't any difference in the results from one person to another. But in reality, nothing could be further from the truth. In the same vein, it's just not effective leadership when people are promoted based on how nice someone is or how long they've been at a company rather than upon specific results.
>
> To help illustrate the point that too much corporate emphasis is on making people feel good rather than emphasizing real leadership, let's discuss Sturgeon's Law—that 90 percent of everything is simply crud.

This usually got a few snickers of laughter, but David was dead serious.

> That's Sturgeon's Law, which at Indytech we call the first law of decline. As far back as 1870, Benjamin Disraeli wrote, "Books are fatal: they are the curse of the human race. Nine-tenths of existing books are nonsense, and the clever books are the refutation of that nonsense."
>
> This concept is crucial in helping companies turn around. Since 90 percent of anything is crud, likewise 90 percent of the alleged leaders in a company are producing cruddy results. It's not that the people are crud. In fact, they may be part of the 10 percent in other areas, but not in their current role or field.

Understanding Sturgeon's Law helps us study the leadership teams honestly and not be fooled by the endless talk with no results. "When all is said and done, much more is said than ever done." The 10 percent walk while the 90 percent talk.

David looked up from the computer screen, then he stood and stretched. He went to the water cooler and filled a large water bottle. He stood for a moment watching the light begin to rise in the sky.

After another long drink, he sat down and went back to the PowerPoint slides.

When a company fills its leadership team and has no sorting mechanism in place, it is poised for a rapid decline. One of our first tasks in a turnaround is to develop a scoreboard that helps separate the 10 percent from the 90 percent.

Some fields are easier than others. Sales records, for example, quickly identify those who get results from those who don't. The people one may think would be successful are not always the ones who sell. Without a scoreboard, it is practically impossible to separate the two groups. It's not like a leader can go ask the people, because self-delusion is so common that many in the 90 percent emphatically believe they are part of the 10 percent. Only hard-core results reveal the truth.

David closed his laptop and walked around the pool area. *I need to think. Who are the 10 percent? When we're talking about freedom, prosperity, and national leadership, we can't just list out any class or group of people as the 10 percent. We certainly don't want to go back to aristocracy or become even more elitist. We're too far down that path already.*

We need a scoreboard, a way of effectively measuring who are the leaders of today's America—the ones who are most likely to turn things around. Who are they? What's the scoreboard?

David found himself walking over to a small pavilion with running water next to it. He had built several pavilions of different sizes and styles around his estate, some for personal reflection and others for small or larger groups to meet. He loved this small pavilion and the sound of the water cascading over the stones in the nearby fountain. And unlike most of the others, this one was entirely surrounded by trees and shrubs and therefore fully secluded. It was almost something of a personal shrine for him.

Who are the 10 percent? And how can we find them?

3

"In my time it was simply the wealthy," James told the room.

"Hold on, now." John spoke out in an annoyed tone. "What about me? Or my cousin Sam? Or Abraham Clark? A lot of us didn't have any money, and I think we added a little to the whole thing. Don't you?"

"Of course," James admitted. "I need to rephrase—"

"You do that," John told him.

"What I meant to say, and thanks to my esteemed colleague for requiring me to be more precise, is that without the wealthy it could not have happened. We simply would not have won. We needed the wealthy, and so does David and his team."

"What team?" John demanded.

"Well, we'll get to that later. But he's going to need the wealthy, and others. Unless we can help him see the need for getting many of the wealthy involved, the whole project will fail."

James scanned the room. "All right, team, who is the next wealthy person on his schedule?"

David's iPhone distracted him from his pondering. He looked down at the name on the calling screen: Marcus. *Earlier than expected*, David mused.

"Good morning."

"Hey, David. Is it too early to call?"

"No. I've been up for hours. What's on your mind?"

"Well, I was thinking about the San Diego turnaround, and I'm not sure what to do."

"Go ahead..."

"Okay, I've applied the 10 percent scoreboard and gathered a month's worth of data, but I'm running into a strange anomaly. I mean, everyone on the leadership team and the rest of the employees clearly break either into the 90 or the 10 factions, based on their production. Like usual. But there is one woman whom I just can't seem to categorize."

"Why not?"

"Well, this is weird, but her production is low on everything we measure, while it is incredibly high in everything else. I think she knows what we're measuring, and she doesn't want to look productive. So I went back and looked at the data from before we got involved, measuring the same stuff we're measuring now. She was extremely productive beforehand, but then she stopped doing those things once we started measuring them. My question is: why wouldn't she want to look good on our scoring?"

"I've seen this before," David said. "Sometimes it happens because the person already has a job lined up elsewhere and doesn't want to make things more complex. Other times there is some personal issue going on between various employees, like a relationship problem. Could it be either of these?"

"Maybe. She was promoted quickly, has high reviews. Her production didn't go down until we came along, and even then it only went down in the measured areas. A lot of the people I've talked to still see her as one of the top leaders in the company. Nearly everyone wonders what she thinks on important questions."

"What about just asking her?"

"Yeah, that's what I was thinking. But I just wanted to be sure you were good with that approach. I'll be there Wednesday and through the weekend."

"I think being direct is the best approach."

"Thanks for your help, David; I appreciate your feedback."

"Call me after you talk to her, Marcus. I'm really interested. The scoreboards work, but we can nearly always find ways to improve them."

David put away his phone and closed his eyes. He loved the smell of the small, forested area.

Why do some people hold back? George Washington was clearly part of the founding 10 percent, but he repeatedly tried to downplay how much the new nation needed him. He always wanted to retire to Mount Vernon and leave the leadership to others.

David's thoughts turned back to where he had been before his decision last night. *Many of my friends think I am crazy. They say, "C'mon, David, you've reached the point in life where you should enjoy your prosperity and status. Why take on a project of this magnitude when you are financially independent and can enjoy the finer things in life?"*

I have run that question through my head endless times and have come up with the same answer every time—because freedom matters. I love this country, and I fear we are losing our freedoms.

I do know that leaders must design the culture and operating structures to block the advance of the FLD. If we just neglect them, they will work like acid on metal, slowly corroding and eventually eating away the noblest organizations.

I have a message in my heart, and I cannot while away the time without sharing this message with our leaders. Maybe I am crazy, but at least I will be able to sleep at night knowing that I did all I could to help.

David stopped, smiled, and then laughed at himself. *I know it all sounds so dramatic, and even a bit wild.* He had always been able to laugh when his thoughts became too intense.

Then his face turned serious again. *The future of freedom, I believe, hangs in the balance.*

A sudden thought occurred to him, and he punched the speed dial to Marcus.

"Hey. I have question for you. Does the woman in San Diego actually need the job? Is she financially independent or does she have other prospects, even in this economy? If so, she might want to hold back and let you promote other people. Sometimes people who don't really need something—like money, recognition, or whatever—don't feel the need to impress. Call it the George Washington principle."

"I'll find out. Thanks."

David turned on the recorder function of his phone and left himself a note: "The George Washington principle, where the best leaders, the top members of the 10 percent, don't feel the need to impress anyone because they'd be just as happy if somebody else fixed the problems and did the leading.

"To really measure the 10 percent, any analysis of potential national leadership has to account for these people. They're not selfish; they just don't care as much about recognition or money as most people do.

"In fact, this is a huge strength that makes them even more valuable as leaders. Look for them."

4

The two men waved at Josh, then walked out of the screening room and climbed the stairs to the tower. They stood at the railing and scanned the large mall full of buildings. Since all the walls were made of glass, they could see thousands of workers in many rooms.

In the distance they could see the complex dedicated to science, in the other direction the buildings focused on the arts. James nodded toward the large group of buildings they had just left. "We have so many people trying to help spread freedom. But sometimes it seems we accomplish very little. Do you think this time will be different?"

John shook his head. "I don't know," he said slowly. "Change is hard. The history of the world drags on for centuries with little change, then we see major shifts that occur in a few short years. It's hard to predict."

From their vantage point in the tower, they could see hundreds of large screens in the rooms of the buildings. James sighed. "Workers are watching screens, studying everything in history and all that is going on in the world today like it was a modern movie. We can fast-forward or rewind, zoom in, and even see into the thoughts of people. But we can't just reach down and fix things."

"No, but we can keep trying. If you keep an eye on David and send down thoughts and suggestions, he might just rise to his potential. That's what we do all day. And let's be honest, we actually have a lot more influence on building freedom than we did in our time. Admit it, Madison," John said with a dry smile, "being an angel has its perks!"

James grinned in surprise. "Yes, it does," he said with a laugh. He cocked his head to one side. "I wonder if we're using all our resources? I mean, what if it's me who isn't quite living up to my full potential? What if we can do more to reach down and fix things?"

John lifted his gaze and locked eyes with James. Both sensed that this was a significant moment.

*T*he Founders got it wrong. I mean, they got so much right, but somehow they thought that creating the right political and legal systems was going to be enough. But they needed to mix the right economic system into the governmental structure.

David was up again the next night at two a.m., reading through his library and writing his main thoughts. Now that he was openly committed to this project, he found that thoughts kept coming to him in a stream throughout the day and night. He needed to get these thoughts down on paper.

The Founding Fathers believed in free enterprise, thankfully, and they helped the process of ending the landed and monied aristocracies that ruined nearly all nations of history; but somehow they needed to work economic freedom more directly into the system.

But how?

David pulled up his Five Laws of Decline PowerPoint and picked up where he had left off the day before.

> The second law describes humanity's desire to satisfy their wants by doing the least amount of work possible. True competition against other companies is the only way to ensure that everyone is working together within a company to satisfy their customers.

If, through guarantees, monopolies, or socialism, one's paycheck is ensured without effort, the majority will do the minimum possible to continue to receive the reward. We first discovered this in Frédéric Bastiat's book, *The Law*.

Bastiat wrote: "Man can live and satisfy his wants only by ceaseless labor; by the ceaseless application of his faculties to natural resources. This process is the origin of property.

"But it is also true that a man may live and satisfy his wants by seizing and consuming the products of the labor of others. This process is the origin of plunder.

"Now since man is naturally inclined to avoid pain—and since labor is pain in itself—it follows that men will resort to plunder whenever plunder is easier than work. History shows this quite clearly. And under these conditions, neither religion nor morality can stop it.

"When, then, does plunder stop? It stops when it becomes more painful and more dangerous than labor."

Plunder can be as simple as receiving a check without working, or as big as one country invading another to receive the fruits of another's labor. Either way the desire is within the heart of man and must be accounted for. In other words, each system must be designed with this inherent attribute in mind, or the organization will decline when people find ways to resort to plunder rather than productivity.

In short, having competition and a scoreboard against other firms is the only way to ensure a team is performing rather than plundering.

David stopped reading the slides and turned his thoughts to modern America. *Clearly, we have become a society addicted to various kinds of plunder. Government entitlements and programs are literally bankrupting our nation, and they keep growing no matter what happens in elections. Whether Republicans or Democrats are in office, government spending consistently increases.*

And sadly, many of the people, for their part, are committed to plunder as well. If they think there is an easier way than working, such as going on a reality show or entering a lottery, they flock to it. For most Americans, education is now less about learning or gaining knowledge than about ensuring higher pay and better perks of employment.

If we are going to turn America around, we've got to address this reality. As long as our system encourages various types of plunder rather than making work the easiest way to succeed, we'll continue to decline. No politician or political party can do anything against this truth.

David looked back at his screen:

The third law of decline works closely with the second. When the second law is violated, the third law, Gresham's Law, becomes automatically engaged.

Thomas Gresham, an English financier, first elaborated Gresham's Law as it pertains to money. He taught that when a government uses force to support one kind of currency over another, the bad money drives out the good.

But Gresham's Law applies to more than just money. In short, when a bad behavior is rewarded, more of the bad behavior will be done, and that in turn will drive out the good behaviors.

In the leadership field, this is displayed when bad behavior is rewarded. For example, if someone can sit at their desk all day watching movies and get paid, this will cause others to choose this simpler method of making money (plunder).

Rewarding bad behaviors either converts others to plunder or drives them out of the company as they seek a firm that rewards people based upon productivity, not plunder. In any case, over time, all that is left at the company are people who choose plunder over productivity—and Gresham's Law strikes again.

These laws (Bastiat and Gresham) must be neutralized or they will quickly strengthen and reinforce each other, and make everything worse.

America is a living example of Gresham's Law, David pondered. *And both Bastiat's Law and Gresham's Law make it a lot harder to identify the 10 percent who have leadership power and can turn things around.*

David pushed away from his desk and climbed the stairs to his deck in the clock tower. He sat on a couch and scanned the horizon. He loved this vantage point, mainly for the view but also for the quiet—no phones, computers, television screens, or other electronic distractions.

As he looked out above the tops of the trees and across the bay, he came back to his earlier concern.

How can we get the 10 percent engaged?

Yes, we have hurt the American monetary system by going off the gold standard, and yes, we have hurt the American work ethic by allowing various kinds of legal plunder to spread in our society. We have also become a nation that rewards lazy or, even worse, unscrupulous behavior in many ways.

All of that is true. But the 10 percent leadership solutions aren't going to be found in Bastiat's Law or Gresham's Law. Plunder is our symptom, not the cause of our national decline. In the case of modern America, the lack of great leadership is clearly the most glaring problem I've encountered so far.

That said, I've learned something in my decades of doing turnarounds: the leaders are always there. We just have to find them and get them to find the courage to step forward and lead.

Where will the leaders come from in our time?

5

"James, time is getting short."

"Yes, sir. I know. We've got a lead . . . a very promising lead, sir."

"I've been following it. And I think you're right. His progress is impressive. My concern is more about your team."

"Really, sir? I don't quite understand. I think we can help him get the answers he needs. He's right on track, sir."

"Yes, James, he is. But have you considered how your team is going to get the answers we need—from him? I have no doubt you can help him. But can he help us? That is the larger question."

James felt his mind racing. This was going to be harder than he thought.

All 100 percent of the people must have their rights protected, and everyone must be treated equally before the law. But Sturgeon's Law is real—10 percent of the people are going to lead the nation and take it in whatever direction they end up choosing. So we've got to find a way to get the right 10 percent of the population leading our nation.

"And we've got to do it soon, since the Laws of Decline have been increasing their influence with each passing decade. We don't have a lot of time left."

"I agree with you, David," Marcus said. "But why are you telling me all this? I've been using the Five Laws of Decline for years with you in business turnarounds all over North America, and I think I know them pretty much as well as you do. I just don't know how you think you're going to turn around the entire country.

"Let's be honest. One of our first rules is that we don't turn around organizations that don't want to be fixed. We aren't hostile-takeover experts. We work with people who *want* to make things right. They don't always want to do everything we tell them, but they do want the end goal of a positive and lasting solution. I just don't think the government really wants to change that much. Or if it does, it's mainly to put its own party in power."

"Maybe that's true, Marcus, but our government isn't the whole company. The government is just the current leadership team. The company—the board of directors of America, if you will—is the people, the citizens, all of us. And the people do want a turnaround. They want a real fix, and they're starting to feel desperate."

Marcus considered this. "That's a good point," he said. "In fact, you could make the case that the government consists of groups of competing hostile-takeover artists all trying to get more power."

"And the people—the real stakeholders in the company that is America—they want a real solution."

"Yes. I see that. And following that logic, the number one need is to find out who the truly productive leaders are so we can help the citizens build an effective leadership team."

"Right," David said.

"Okay, then," Marcus continued. "The first step is to create an effective scoreboard to measure and determine who the real leaders of America are."

"Yes. That's where I'm stuck."

Marcus stared. "That's shocking. I've never heard you say you are stuck—on anything. Especially not on analyzing how to score leadership and productivity in a company."

"Well, here's the problem," David said into the screen. "You. You are the problem. You, Marcus, are the reason I'm stuck."

For the second time in one day, Marcus was stunned.

"Me?" he asked.

"Let me ask you: what kind of watch are you wearing?" David asked.

Surprised by the change of subject, Marcus glanced down at his wrist. "Uh, it's a Ulysse Nardin GMT. Why?"

"Tell me more," David said.

"About what?"

"About the watch."

"Oh, well, it's the 322-66 Limited Edition, and I got it—"

"That's enough. Now tell me about that Tag watch you were wearing last week."

"Uh. Okay. It was a Tag Heuer Grand Carrera titanium chronograph with caliper and..."

"Great." David paused. "Now tell me about Article I, Section 8 of the U.S. Constitution."

"Um..."

"I'll wait. Take your time. But tell me details."

Marcus laughed. "Look, I'm no political scholar," he said.

They laughed together. Then David replied, "Neither am I, Marcus. But that's my point. You and I are the problem. I can tell you intricate details about various leadership books and management theories, and you can, too. I can tell you a lot about real estate, investment, finance, and a bunch of other topics. And you can tell me things I'll never want to know about watches, cars, and the fabric of suits. And if our partner Bob were here, he could tell us crazy-deep details about tennis, and Monte could go on and on about horse breeding.

"The thing is, Marcus, all of that is great. That's what freedom is all about. I can love leadership and real estate, you can love watches and cars, and all our friends can have their interests, hobbies, careers, and areas of expertise. So don't get me wrong—I think it's wonderful that you like high-quality watches. You've worked hard, and you deserve to spend your money on the things you really like.

"Again, freedom makes it possible for everyone to do the same. But that's my whole point. We have freedom today because many people in the past knew as much about freedom as I know about business turnarounds and you know about watches. In fact, a lot of people had to know the principles of freedom in depth, or we would never have become free.

"But today we're losing it all. Very few people really know about freedom, and too many of those who are experts on the history of freedom aren't even focused on citizenship or protecting our freedom. So, yes, we need a new 10 percent to truly lead a national turnaround, and we need it soon.

"And you and I are part of the problem. And everybody else like us, who know a lot about their careers and other interests but who know little about freedom. I know enough to know that this is how freedom is lost, and once it is lost it takes blood, pain, and massive sacrifice to get it back."

Marcus was nodding by now, so David stopped to catch his breath. After a short silence, he looked up at the screen to see Marcus smiling. "What?" he asked.

"You know."

"I do?"

"Yes. I'm in. Let's do this. Let's give America the old turn-around treatment."

6

"Mr. President, they really need Miss Stone."

"I know," James said, "but she's so different from them. I just don't know if they'll feel comfortable working with her."

"They'll fail without her, Mr. President."

"I know."

D avid put the chair into the recline position and pulled out his laptop. It was a six-hour flight, and he wanted to get back to his crazy "Save the U.S." project.

The last two weeks had been so busy, and both David and Marcus had been hoping to hear from each other with some big breakthrough on the 10 percent. But so far . . . nothing.

David opened his PowerPoint and began reading:

The fourth law works on the other side, after a firm has achieved a level of success. The Law of Diminishing Returns (LDR) states that even if a company executes properly on the first three laws, eventually it will get big enough that the fourth law will engage.

The Law of Diminishing Returns states, "To continue without significant changes after a certain level of performance has been reached will result in a decline in effectiveness." In other words, if a company achieves success, it will continue to grow until it reaches the LDR—*where increased quantity produces lessened quality.*

For example, a restaurant that is successful can quickly become unsuccessful by expanding too fast and experiencing the LDR effect. Quality demands a culture of excellence, and this takes time and the right people (10 percent) to implement it.

When quantities, growth, or size increase without accounting for LDR, quality decreases. Mass media, mass education, mass transportation, mass art, mass technology, and mass government, among other things, have all experienced the LDR. Increased quantities frequently decrease the quality of the products produced.

David turned to the traveler in the next seat and asked, "Do you think our government is too big?"

A little surprised by the directness of the question, the man turned to humor him. "My mother taught me never to discuss politics or religion in polite company."

They both laughed, and David apologized for being so direct. "I'm just working on a project, and I'm so sure the government has grown so big and bloated that I can't imagine any American not agreeing with me."

"Well, I don't disagree with you," the man replied. "That's certainly the conservative view."

"Actually," David said, "I'm an independent. I don't have much faith in political parties."

"I hear you." The man was warming up to the conversation. "To tell the truth, I'm an independent, too. But when I hear people talk about government being too big, it often feels like they're happy spending whatever they want on international conflicts but don't want to pay for real needs here in the U.S."

"Well, I'm sure we could point out flaws with both parties, but I don't want to get political. I just wonder how many people think the government is too big."

"Let's find out," the man said as he pulled out his laptop. "I'll check out Gallup."

Both men surfed for a few minutes, then the man said, "Well, in one Gallup poll 59 percent of Americans said the government is too big, and in another one fully 81 percent of those polled were dissatisfied with the federal government."

"Thanks," David said. "What about you? I'm really interested in what you think."

"Well, okay. I'll be honest. I do think government is too big, but I don't like this question very much because I think those on the Right will use my answer to justify the things they want to cut while those on the Left will do the same. Both sides want to cut some things and spend more on other things."

"Yeah," David agreed, "but isn't that the whole point? They both want to cut less than they want to increase spending, or at least that is what happens even when they say they're going to balance things."

The man nodded. "That's for sure. Election after election, we hear big promises, some good and some bad, but no matter whom we elect, the government spending just goes up."

"That's called the Law of Diminishing Returns," David said.

After a long discussion, David turned back to his laptop. He scanned various polls of the American people that reflected their growing frustrations with government. Then he opened the Power-Point window and read:

> The final and fifth law marries all the previous laws together and is a product of the inertia they have created. The Law of Inertia, in laymen's terms, states, "An object at rest tends to stay at rest, and an object in motion tends to stay in motion."

If, in other words, the first four laws are in motion, it is extremely difficult to turn them around without massive surgery to remove the wrong leaders and wrong systems, all wrongly rewarded.

Imagine a pool where all the children have swum in the same direction for ten laps. If an adult were to jump in the pool and run against the current, she would experience the debilitating effect of the Law of Inertia. The current would push against her and literally take her backward, even though she may be doing the right things and moving in the right direction.

It's much easier to keep a company moving in the right direction than it is to turn around a company that is moving in the wrong direction. This is why companies pay so much for turnaround specialists, because it is the toughest task in leadership to turn around a company against negative inertia.

David leaned back, closed his eyes, and began to summarize his thoughts on the Five Laws of Decline.

I remember my "Aha" moment when the FLD meshed with my understanding of history. I was shocked by how well the FLD described the fall of Rome. I had studied and learned these principles for business, but only later did I realize how fitting they were for nations, churches, and businesses.

Studying the history of Rome was where I had my breakthrough. Rome progressed through the early kings into a republic, and later morphed into a dictatorship as the plunder gained from wars caused all five laws to engage.

1. *Sturgeon's Law*—90 percent of the Roman politicians and senators were crud. Most weren't leaders and looked only for ease and comfort. Others looked for illicit gains made possible by the powerful Roman army.

2. *Bastiat's Law* is the hinge that swings the door of the Five Laws. When Rome defeated Carthage, Rome's first satellite territory produced grain and income for the Romans. For the first time Bastiat's Law clouded the minds of the hardworking Romans, who began to enjoy money and food gathered without effort. The Romans, as all people, liked the idea, and they initiated wider wars to bring more cities and kingdoms into the Roman fold.

3. *Gresham's Law* drove out the noble characters in politics, because they would not play the power games needed to thrive in the newly corrupt Rome. Leadership of Rome no longer was based on duty and honor, but instead upon desire to control the means of force to plunder outlying possessions. This brought more Machiavellian characters into Rome, and with the death of both Cato the Younger and Cicero, Gresham's Law was fully realized.

4. *The Law of Diminishing Returns* kicked in when, through continuous expansion, Rome grew from a city to an empire extending across much of Eurasia and Northern Africa. Neither the Senate nor, later, the Caesars were capable of leading such a vast area of varying cultures and nations. With the plunder from numerous lands entering Rome, the local citizens were bought off with bread and circuses, bringing the decline of the Roman citizens as well as their government.

5. *The Law of Inertia* made things so bad at the end of the empire that the people hardly resisted as the barbarian hordes overran their city. Rome was exhausted under its own weight of decline at work. In truth, many of the citizens no longer felt the Roman way was worth saving, with taxes, regulations, and plunder at unsustainable heights.

Rome fell, in other words, because it first opened the door to the Five Laws of Decline by governing territories. Furthermore, instead of closing the door, it swung the door wide open until it drove out the older Roman virtues and replaced them with greed for money and power.

The Five Laws cannot be negotiated with—either a business or nation kills the FLD, or the FLD will kill it. The Egyptian, Greek, Roman, Spanish, French, German, and English empires all fell due to the entropic effects of the Five Laws of Decline, while America is badly sick from the same cause. The question for us is, "Is it too late?"

As the plane began its descent, David felt a twinge of the old sense of frustration that had plagued him for months—until he had decided to do something about it for good. Now, after days of feeling stuck, it was starting to return.

"The inertia must be turned around, and that means leadership," he said aloud.

"What's that?" the man in the next seat asked.

David look at him and smiled. "You're one of the 10 percent," he said.

"Maybe," the man said. "Thanks for teaching me about Sturgeon's Law, and the other four, too. This was an interesting conversation."

"I wonder how many of these people on the plane are part of the 10 percent?" David mused.

"More than you know," said the man.

Something in the man's voice made David turn and look at him more closely. The man smiled through his freckles and red hair.

"Sorry, we talked for half the flight and I never introduced myself. I'm David."

"Hi, David," the man said. "I'm James."

7

"They're about to meet, Mr. President."

"Good. Now, about the other thing . . . ?"

"Well, Mr. President, I have some ideas, but I don't think you're going to like them. Or even believe them."

This is Kami Stone," Marcus said.

"Hello." David smiled. "Marcus has told me a lot about you."

"Really?" Kami asked. "That's a surprise."

David liked the way Kami presented herself, and he decided to get right to the point.

"Why did you reduce your production in everything we measured and increase it in the things we weren't measuring?" he asked with a warm smile.

Kami didn't miss a beat. "Because I was measuring how good you are as leaders."

Marcus and David looked at each other.

"Well, what have you discovered?" Marcus asked.

"I'm still deciding, but this conversation shows promise."

David loved a challenge. "If you were in charge, Kami, what would we do next?"

A big smile spread across her face. "Okay, fine, I'll take the job. But I don't need it, so if you give it to me allow me the time and flexibility to do it right. I only ask one thing: tell me straight out what results you want from the company under my leadership, and I'll tell you whether or not—and when—I can deliver them."

Both men were surprised, which made Kami's smile get even bigger.

"Kami, I've seen bravado before, and I've seen confidence that didn't end in productivity, so how can we measure your productivity before we jump?" David asked.

"Give me one week to produce on your scoreboard, and let's talk again," Kami said.

"Okay. But since I won't be here in person next week, tell me what makes you tick."

"Mr. Mersher." She looked him directly in the eyes. "I care about freedom, and I will do my best to spread it as far and wide as possible."

It was David's turn to be shocked. This was certainly an unexpected answer. On the one hand the answer had little to do directly with the business, but on the other hand it was exactly what David wanted to hear—though he hadn't known it before she said it.

Marcus was warming up to this conversation. "Miss Stone, what do you know about this watch I'm wearing?" he asked.

She looked at it like she hadn't noticed it before, which for some reason made David smile, then said, "Not much. I know the Jaeger-LeCoultre brand is nearly on par with Breguet, Patek Philippe, and Muller, and I know the JLCs hold their value well. But, like I said, I don't know a lot about watches."

"Well, that's not a bad answer." Marcus was all smiles. "Now, what do you know about Article I, Section 8 of the United States Constitution?"

"Well, I'm not sure why you're asking, but that's where the twenty powers of Congress are enumerated. It's kind of like the engine of the Constitution, the list of things the federal government can do. Madison taught that this list was also a limitation on the central government, because it couldn't do anything not included on the list. Most of the *Federalist Papers*—after the first twenty, which give a general introduction to the Constitution—argue the validity of these powers. Do you want me to list the twenty?"

Marcus was deeply surprised, but he managed to keep a straight face. "No, Miss Stone, that won't be necessary." He looked at David in shock, then asked business questions for the next forty minutes.

David sat back and listened carefully, but his mind was racing. *The man on the plane, and now this. The 10 percent are out there, just like they always are in a business. If we can find them and empower them, we really can turn the nation around. I'm so glad I came to San Diego today.*

How do we find the 10 percent? What's the scoreboard? It's time to call Monte.

David excused himself and left Marcus and Kami to their interview. He punched #2 on the speed dial, and his phone called Monte. The #1 on his speed dial was reserved for Amy.

While the phone rang, David thought about Monte and their long years together.

Monte Christensen was Indytech's president. He oversaw the entire operation and answered only to David, the CEO. He had been David's first partner when they founded the company together. Monte was a former race car driver, but that career ended when he was injured in an accident. During the lean years at the beginning, David and Monte had been the only full-time employees—consulting, managing, planning, keeping records, taking out the trash, and everything else.

As the company grew and eventually flourished, Monte had returned to his passion of racing, but this time by breeding thoroughbreds. Horses were his passion, and he could relate any business problem to a horse race. Monte and his wife, Michelle, were the Mershers' best friends, and the four of them could be found doing things business or social almost daily. David and Amy affectionately referred to Monte and Michelle as the M&Ms.

"Hi, Monte. I'm in San Diego today. Marcus and I are having

some excellent meetings, but I just can't stop thinking about this freedom project I've assigned to myself. I've reached a roadblock, and I can't seem to get past it. I've been stuck in a rut on this for weeks now, and I could really use your creativity and insight. Do you have a few minutes?"

"Sure," Monte said. "What's the problem?"

"Well, as you know, I'm applying the Five Laws of Decline to the United States, and it's experiencing all five in massive doses. As I analyze the details, it becomes clear that we need improvements on all five levels, but that the biggest need is to find the 10 percent who can effectively lead a turnaround. I'm convinced that the 10 percent exist, but I can't figure out how to find them—what's the right scoreboard to identify them?

"Like I said, I've been struggling with this for weeks, but so far I haven't figured it out. What do you think, Monte?"

"That's a big one, David. Like trying to win the Triple Crown every year for a decade. So let's run the numbers. We have a little over 300 million people in America, so 10 percent is at least 30 million. You could argue that the 10 percent has to bring freedom for the whole world, which would make the 10 percent to around 700 million—"

David cut him off. "I'd stick with the U.S. numbers. American freedom certainly influences the world, but the leadership team for a U.S. turnaround is going to be pretty much all Americans."

"So just the main event," Monte mused. "Okay, so 30 million, right?"

"Well, we could stick with adults, which would cut the 10 percent down to around 25 million people. Not that kids don't make a difference—they do—but I think our 10 percent should at least be eligible to vote."

"Well, I read that about 58 percent of those eligible actually vote in presidential elections, and that's on a good year. So that brings your number of 250 million U.S. adults down to 145 million, and probably around 5 million of them are unavailable for leadership, for various reasons. Half of those are incarcerated, for example. • That brings your number to about 140 million, so we are looking for about 14 million Americans to lead the turnaround."

"That's a lot."

"Yes, it is." Monte sighed deeply. "It's way too many. I mean, you and I both know that we can't use Sturgeon's Law of 10 percent to turn things around by breaking the Law of Diminishing Returns right at the start. Your number of 14 million is just too big to avoid diminishing returns. It's unmanageable."

"That's my dilemma," David affirmed. "I haven't been able to get past that. I've reworked the numbers over and over, but this is where the scoreboard always breaks down. In business, if it's too big, we break things into smaller internal units with their own leadership. How do you do that with a nation?

"Of course, the Founders already thought of that when they put limits on the federal government and left most of the power to the states or the people, but in current America that plan isn't working. We want to get back to that system, yes, but it won't work as a turnaround as long as the states are simply treated by Washington as mere appendages of the central government."

"So we're stuck with the need for a 10 percent leadership team that is just too big. David, that really is a challenge…"

"So it's a challenge. I know. But what's the solution? I know there is one. What is it?"

Both men pondered silently for a few moments.

"Who's with you right now?" Monte asked.

"Well, Marcus is interviewing candidates for the 10 percent here at our San Diego client, so it's just Marcus and me."

"We need a mastermind meeting, don't you think?"

David considered it. "That's a really good idea," he said slowly, "and Marcus just introduced me to someone who might be part of it."

8

"They're meeting, and Miss Stone is part of it, Mr. President."

"All six of them are there?"

"Yes, Mr. President. Three in person and Mrs. Mersher, and Mr. and Mrs. Christensen, on Skype."

James laughed at the word Skype. *What an amazing world these people lived in.*

"Okay, Josh. Assemble the team."

As you all know," David began, "a mastermind allows all of us to deal with a challenge as a team and create an environment of synergy where our combined mind power is greater than anything we could do separately." He then brought them up to speed on the whole project, right down to the need for an effective scoreboard to find the 10 percent who could lead America's turnaround. He put the numbers on the whiteboard and outlined the conflict between Sturgeon's Law and the Law of Diminishing Returns.

"Let's figure this out," he said, just before he sat down.

Everyone stared at the whiteboard.

After a few moments of silence, David chuckled. "This isn't a very good start, is it?"

His infectious humor reached everyone, and the whole room smiled.

David scanned the room, and he could tell that Kami wanted to say something. "What do you think, Kami?" he prompted.

"Well, I'm new here," she said, "but the word that comes to mind is *constraints*."

"*The Theory of Constraints*, by Eli Goldratt. Great book," Marcus responded.

"It certainly applies here," Monte said. "The five steps of focus, the process of change, and how to invent simple solutions for complex problems."

"Yes," Amy added, "and we clearly see that our bottleneck is finding the 10 percent when the number is too big to be effective."

"Right." David's mind was moving too fast for his words. "We must be sure our solution isn't just a quick fix. And we can benefit from a Current Reality Tree, where identifying all of the facts in this challenge of fixing America might help us identify the roots and causes—and therefore the solutions."

"I think the key point here is finding simple solutions to seemingly complex problems," Monte said. "Remember how Goldratt does this? He says that all complex problems are actually made simple in three ways. First, we have to stop assuming that the solution is complex and instead assume that there is an astonishingly simple solution that we just haven't found yet."

"Agreed," said David.

"Second, we should stop thinking of conflicts as a given, and instead ask how the two sides can work together."

"So," Marcus broke in, "the 10 percent and the huge numbers aren't actually in conflict. Somehow, they are natural allies. We just have to figure out in what universe 14 million people on a leadership team is a nice, manageable number."

Everyone laughed.

"Actually," Kami said, "when I interned with a policy institute they routinely talked about millions of people and trillions of dollars as if these were nice, small, manageable numbers. Then when I went into business these same numbers were seen as big and complex."

"But they are too big," David said. "The Law of Diminishing Returns is real..."

"Yes, it is...but what if it wasn't?" Kami said firmly. "Seriously, what if it wasn't too big? What universe would that be? What would it look like? We need to think outside the box, right?"

Everyone pondered, then Monte said, "Okay, is it possible that these numbers aren't too big? That somehow, some way, they are just right? Let's just say this is true, just for the sake of argument. If it is true, if 14 million leaders aren't too many, what would the circumstances have to be?"

"Let's frame the question like this." Amy paused. "What would make 14 million the perfect, nice, manageable number of leaders for an effective and excellent turnaround of the United States?"

Kami stood up and erased the whiteboard, then she wrote Amy's question on it in big letters. Everyone read and reread the words.

"I hope this won't take us off track," Monte said, "but the third way to make a complex question simple is to stop blaming our business partners and to stop underestimating their abilities and insight. I think this really applies in this case. All Americans tend to underestimate each other, and to blame the voting public for being duped or shallow. Goldratt says that not only does this blind us from the real solutions, but it also allows our emotions to get in the way of success; as long as we think that regular American citizens can't lead this thing, our scoreboard will be flawed."

David was experiencing one epiphany after another. "So," he said excitedly, "if we think that Sturgeon's Law is actually that only 10 percent or fewer can really lead, we'll miss the point. There really are millions of people who can lead this turnaround. We can't think that there aren't enough of them, because Sturgeon's Law is real. We just need to believe it, even when it says that there are already millions of leaders who can lead this thing!"

"The 14 million may be unmanageable," Kami said slowly, "but it isn't too big."

Something was nagging David, and years of leading this kind of discussion had taught him to listen to such feelings, even when his excitement was leading him in a different direction.

Decades of learned discipline kicked in, and he sat back and analyzed the whole group. *What am I missing?*

Then it dawned on him. Masterminds work to their highest potential *only* when everyone got involved.

"We haven't heard from you yet, Michelle," David said. "What are your thoughts so far?"

Michelle shifted in her seat and leaned in toward the camera. "I keep thinking that...well, let me put it this way...Every time someone mentions that 14 million is unmanageable, I keep feeling that it would be a tragedy to try to manage them at all.

"The founding generation wasn't really managed, was it? Different leaders did different things, and it all came together. Sometimes it looked managed, but most of the time it looked like chaos. But somehow, despite the chaos, it worked. Millions of people took action together, each in his or her own way, and the result was freedom."

Everyone was nodding, so Michelle kept talking. "Today, millions take action, but how many of them are taking action to try to get America back on track? Probably a lot, but probably not 14 million every day. We've got to stop thinking of this like a business, like Kami said, and start seeing this as a nation of people. Very smart and capable people who all want the right thing. And at least 14 million of them are able to make the needed change, if they could just all get to work. It would look like chaos, but it would work..."

Michelle paused, then added: "And if anybody tries to manage it all, it won't work. That's what the political parties do, and at times the media or other groups. We don't need to be managed; we need to realize how much power we have and just get to work—individually and in small groups."

David sat in stunned silence. The conversation continued, but he had stopped paying attention. *That's it. She's right.*

"Maybe the scoreboard isn't something we use to measure," David said, "to be analyzed by turnaround experts who then call in the top performers and assign them leadership. We've got to think bigger. The scoreboard is simpler than all that. Maybe the scoreboard is self-scored, something we put out there and leave to the 10 percent to find and apply on their own, in their own way. If they're part of the 10 percent, and if we put out the right scoreboard, they'll see it and do something about it.

"It will look like chaos, like Michelle said, but it will work."

Kami stood up and walked to the whiteboard. "What should I write?" she asked.

David looked at Michelle, and everyone else followed his lead.

"I think," Michelle said, "you should write three things:

1. The leaders are out there.
2. They are smart, strong, and up to this task.
3. The scoreboard must simply call them to action, not manage them."

David stood and picked up another marker, then he added to the whiteboard:

1. The leaders are out there (10 percent).
2. They are smart, strong, and up to this task (Bastiat's Law).
3. The scoreboard must call them to action, not manage them (Law of Inertia).

HOW DO WE CREATE A SCOREBOARD THAT EFFECTIVELY CALLS THEM TO ACTION?

He sat down without saying anything.

"Is it time for a break?" Monte asked the group.

9

"*Thank you all,*" *James told the team.* "*That was good work. What's the plan for the next hour?*"

Josh raised his hand. "*I think we should guide them in the direction of amending the Constitution, returning things to a better balance.*"

Many nodded. Josh continued, "*For example, we could return more power to the states and communities by—*"

James held up his hand. "*Sorry, Josh. We don't have a lot of time, and I need to say something. I've been thinking about this for weeks now, and I'm convinced this is about more than our team helping inspire a fix for David's world. We need to let David and his team inspire us to fix the world of our time.*"

James had known this moment would come, and he had wondered how the group would take it, but he was surprised by the number of gasps and looks of shock from the team.

Kami splashed water on her face and wiped it with a towel. Her makeup smeared slightly, but she quickly fixed it and then stood looking into the mirror. She hated makeup, anyway.

The meeting was going well, she thought, but she was trying too hard to fit in. She knew she needed to relax, that the best way to impress these people was to not try to be impressive. But she really liked this group, and she wanted to work with them long-term.

Why am I so insecure? This is so frustrating. They're such a tight-knit group, she lamented. *Still, they seemed to value my input more than other places I've worked. I'm coming across like a know-it-all. I always do this—and I have to stop!*

The big problem was that Kami knew what needed to happen. Or, at least, she knew part of what was needed. "Watch out, it's easier done than said!" she joked to the mirror. She laughed at her play on words, then grew serious.

The answers were there, but how to help this group see it? She'd been thinking about this topic for years, poring over the great books, classics of the world, writings of the Founders and other great thinkers throughout history, and carefully taking notes as she developed a plan to reenergize freedom in the world.

But she couldn't just pass out her plan. The group had to arrive at its own conclusions. Besides, she was learning a lot from the group—the plan would be much better as a joint effort.

I need to learn more from these people, she told herself. Kami took a deep breath and walked back into the conference room.

"Okay, let's get started," David announced. "I think we should begin by brainstorming ways to create a call to action for the 10 percent."

"May I make a comment?" Kami asked. "I think it's important to recognize that we aren't talking about just one kind of leader when we say 'the 10 percent.'"

Seeing that she had everyone's attention, she continued, "On one level, since this will look like the chaos Michelle talked about, every member of the 10 percent will lead in their own unique way. So, in a sense, we actually need to create a call to action for millions of different types of leaders.

"But, on a more realistic level, at least three kinds of leaders are needed. I told David and Marcus before that I see my life's mission as spreading freedom, and I've been thinking about how to increase

American and world freedom for many years. Maybe some of what I've learned can help our discussion."

Kami paused, but David nodded to her to keep talking. "Okay," she said, "first let me say that I'm struggling with the numbers we are using. I don't disagree with Sturgeon's Law of 10 percent, but let's talk briefly about the numbers.

"Before Sturgeon's Law, which was articulated in the 1950s, came the Pareto Principle in 1906. The Italian economist Vilfredo Pareto noted in that year that 20 percent of the populace owned 80 percent of the land.

"Over time, this came to be known as the 80/20 Rule. Author Richard Koch wrote *The 80/20 Principle*, where he argued that 80 percent of the people accomplish 20 percent of all productivity and a mere 20 percent of the people accomplish 80 percent of the productivity. He further said that 20 percent of our actions bring 80 percent of our successes, and so on.

"Gallup polls show that about 20 percent of people love their careers and lives, and *Harvard Business Review* ran an article showing that around 20 percent of customers account for about 80 percent of revenue in some companies.

"As scientists, mathematicians, and economists have run the specific numbers in various studies, they have found that Pareto's 80/20 rule is actually closer to Sturgeon's 90/10 model, but that the actual numbers vary depending on what is being studied.

"In other words, the principle of the few swaying the many holds true, but the specific numbers fluctuate slightly. Researchers have argued that the official number should be 72/28, 80/20, 90/10, 95/5, and even 99/1.

"In any case, Sturgeon's Law holds, but we don't have to get too caught up on specific numbers. As closely as I can figure from my own reading and studying what little data is available, in political circles, specifically major changes in society, from revolutions like 1789 France and 1905 Russia to major reformations like the Magna Carta or the American founding, the number is often closer to 97/3.

"That is, around 3 percent takes an active part in changing society in major political, economic, and social ways. In the American founding, about 90,000 people actually took part in leading and fighting for the changes between 1776 and 1789.

"Beyond that, about 300,000 openly supported the American Revolution. Since the colonial population was around 3 million, that's about 10 percent who openly supported the American founding and about 3 percent who took an active lead.

"Other major societal changes follow this same pattern, except when war covers the whole land—like during the Civil War, when of course the rate of participation goes up."

Kami looked around, and everyone was still focused and interested.

"So, to sum up, I think we're dealing with a smaller number than 14 million leaders. Yes, around 30 million will need to openly support the solutions that our leaders implement, and many voters will need to show their support at the voting booth, but the leadership team can be smaller.

"Now, I agree with Michelle that we don't want anybody to manage these leaders—they need to be committed citizens acting for their love of freedom, prosperity, and good values."

Kami noticed that most of the group was nodding, but Monte looked pensive. "Monte, do you have a thought?" she asked.

"Only that reaching any large number can be difficult," Monte said. "We can't use a mass approach—we have to find a way to target the right people."

"I agree." Kami nodded. "But note that the message we'll need to use should appeal to all Americans, not just some special group. The leaders, as Sturgeon's Law and the Pareto Principle assure us, will come from *all* locales, ethnicities, creeds, economic classes, social strata, and age groups. This will only work if it's a truly American leadership, made up of leaders from all walks of life."

"It can't be elitist," Marcus said.

"Right," Kami responded. "And in truth Sturgeon's Law has an elitist bent to it. But if the 10 percent come from across the nation and represent all groups, which is in fact exactly what Sturgeon's Law predicts, then we'll have the kind of leadership we saw during the founding era."

"Or better," David said.

10

Everyone in Josh's team cheered.

"It's working, Mr. President," Josh said.

"It's too soon to be sure," James responded. "But this is certainly a good start. In my day we combined the two opposing forces of aristocracy and democracy by creating a Senate and a House, the first for the elites and the second to represent the masses. They're figuring out how to do something similar."

"It's exciting to see them applying the proven principles in new ways, Mr. President."

"Maybe." James smiled. "We're far from real success. Let's keep our focus."

I have one more thing to add, then I'll stop talking so much," Kami said self-consciously.

"Please, go on," David assured her. "This material is invaluable."

"Well," Kami continued, "there are at least three major groups of leaders that are needed. We've already spoken of the largest group, the many millions who don't have to take direct action in the turnaround but do have to openly support its aims."

"Can we lay off the numbers?" Amy asked. "I'm following them, but I think we've reached a point where too much focus on numbers is distracting from the point. In addition to good citizens, we need a smaller group of leaders, right? But of those leaders, what are the two other groups you mentioned?"

"Good idea, Amy," Kami said. "One of my mentors in college called the three groups of leaders the citizens, the entrepreneurs, and the statesmen.

"The citizens read and think widely and deeply, and they understand the principles of freedom upon which societal success depends. They closely watch society and make their influence felt wherever the need arises. Call this group *citizen-leaders*.

"The second group, or entrepreneurial sector, builds business ventures and helps spread freedom in society by creating prosperity and spreading the entrepreneurial values of initiative, innovation, and tenacity. Call this group *entrepreneurial-leaders* or *social-leaders*.

"The third type of leader understands the principles of freedom deeply, at the level of James Madison, Thomas Jefferson, and the greatest leaders and statesmen of history. They dedicate their lives to studying freedom in great depth and detail. Call this group *statesmen-leaders*, or the New Madisons and Jeffersons.

"Citizens, entrepreneurs, statesmen. All leaders. And all three are needed. We don't need to strategize for all the citizens; we just need to get the 10 percent on track, as David said at the very beginning today.

"One more thing," Kami added. "Manageable leadership does matter in all this, because the Law of Diminishing Returns is very, very real, as we already discussed. So, and this is the variable in the whole project, any one group, like this one, can build what it deems most effective to bring about a high-quality American turnaround, but ultimately it must limit itself to how it can truly lead, and trust others to do their part, too."

David immediately spoke up. "So my goal of a million entrepreneurial-leaders who are financially successful, widely read, and well prepared to lead in society is right on."

He'd said it as a statement, not a question, but Kami responded anyway: "Absolutely."

The members of the group looked around at each other. Marcus spoke. "So we know *who*! And we know *how many*. At least within the ballpark..."

Everyone nodded in agreement.

"...but we still don't know *how*."

"Actually, we do," David said. The group turned to him. "A whole new class of entrepreneurial-minded leaders who are continually reading more, learning more, helping build businesses and communities, and consistently improving their own leadership abilities. That's our goal. That's our vision."

He paused. "Others will have to do their part, but this is our central goal. We've got to do whatever it takes to make this a reality."

"Cool," said Marcus. "This whole freedom thing is way more interesting than I thought it would be."

This brought a laugh from the group, but Monte didn't join in.

"There's more to it than this, David. The 10 percent is our focus, for sure, but it's not the whole thing. We need to do something else."

David rubbed his chin as he considered Monte's words. "Yes, we do," he finally said. "We need a three-part strategy: (a) we need to build the entrepreneurial-leaders; (b) we also need to help find and empower the modern Jeffersons and Madisons; and (c) we need to get the call out to others who will build more entrepreneurial-leaders."

Kami walked to the board, erased everything written on it, and wrote these three.

Everyone looked at the whiteboard. After a few moments of silence, David approached the board, lifted a marker, and wrote in big, bold letters above the three goals:

Vision.

11

"How did your meeting go?"

"I think it went well, sir," James said.

"Did he recognize you?"

"Well, no."

"Actually, that would have been a bit strange if he did. He's not a crackpot, after all."

When the two men stopped laughing, James said thoughtfully, "He's really committed to this. He asked questions about it out of the blue, and I was a total stranger just sitting in the seat as we flew." Then, with a shudder, he continued, "Flying was . . . not a pleasant thing."

This time it was the other man's turn to chuckle. His laughter deepened, and it took him a while to stop.

As he walked back into the hotel boardroom after the break, David heard Marcus intensely explaining something to Kami.

"There are three levels of luxury watches, and a good collection includes watches from each level," Marcus explained. "The third and lowest level includes basic luxury watches like Gucci, Raymond Weil, Chopard, Tag Heuer, and Longines.

"Of course, I say that this is the lowest level, but remember that all three levels are luxury, so they are above premium watches like the high-end Citizen, Guess, Movado, or Bulova."

David smiled as he sat down. He had heard the speech before—it was almost a rite of passage for anyone Marcus wanted to impress.

"The second level of luxury watches includes the popular brands like Rolex, Breitling, Cartier, IWC, and Omega.

"As for the best watches, the first and highest level includes Patek Philippe, Vacheron Constantin, Muller, Richard Mille, Piquet, Zenith, Nardin, Jaeger-LeCoultre, Breguet, and a few others. These are the top level, because many of the watches are individually made by master craftsmen, not run off in a factory like the second and third levels."

"Which brand is your favorite?" Kami asked.

David wondered if she was really interested or was just humoring Marcus, but Marcus didn't seem to have any such concerns. "Tag Heuer," he said without hesitation.

Kami seemed surprised. "Why?"

"You thought it would be one of the first level, didn't you?" He didn't wait for her to answer. "Each brand stands for something, like its main theme or message. And the message says something about the person who wears it. For example, to most people Rolex says, 'rich.' Omega says, 'sophisticated'; Breitling says, 'professional'—"

Kami interrupted him. "What does Tag Heuer say?"

Marcus smiled widely. This was his favorite topic. "Well, first of all, if I did choose a brand from the first level as my favorite, it would be Zenith, because Zenith stands for quality, quality, quality. No marketing. No fanfare. Just quality.

"Now, about Tag Heuer. Many real watch experts don't love Tag Heuer, because it's not sophisticated enough for them, but to me the Tag Heuer brand says, 'maverick, self-made, not trying to fit in, frontier rather than establishment, leader rather than manager, rascal (but the good kind), cutting-edge, avant-garde, entrepreneur rather than part of the system...'" Marcus stopped to take a breath, not because he was finished.

"That's a lengthy motto," she said with a grin.

"Are you mocking me?" Marcus asked with feigned indignity.

"Not at all," she said. "Please go on."

"Please don't," Monte piped up from the screen.

Marcus looked around and saw that everyone was back from the break and ready to reconvene the meeting. Moreover, they were smiling at him.

"Very well," he said sarcastically, "but give me ten seconds to finish." Then, without giving anyone a chance to stop him, he quickly continued, "So, the key to a great watch collection is to keep a balance between all three levels of luxury watches so your collection always has exactly what you need when it's time to put on a watch."

Marcus stood up from his perch on the edge of the table and turned to take his chair. As he sat down Kami said, "I may be getting my geek on, but this kind of reminds me of the three branches of government. Each has its role, and all are important. I know it's a stretch," she said, "but think about it.

"At a deeper level, each has its own kind of leadership— leadership by committee to get things right in the legislative branch, leadership by experts to deal with nuances and disputes through the judicial branch, and leadership in times of challenge along with leadership through symbols in the executive branch."

Kami took a breath, then added, "Or the three levels of government: national, state, and local, all doing their own vital part and none above any other. All equal, all important. At least that's how it was originally, in the time of the Framers." She paused. "Oh, and leadership at each level was different in some very important ways."

David nodded thoughtfully. "That's one of the oldest questions in business. What, precisely, is leadership? If we're going to get the real business leaders more actively involved in governance, we need to clarify what we mean by leadership."

"I agree," Monte said, "but I think leadership includes many important things, as discussed in dozens—hundreds, in fact—of business books. Still, I like Peter Drucker's thought that being a top leader means doing the things nobody else can do. Using that definition, leadership becomes the indispensible action, the thing that only top leaders can accomplish."

"Many things can be delegated," Marcus added, "including most items that are written up in business books as key characteristics of leadership. But there are a few things only true leaders really do, and those are the essence of leadership. For example, I've noticed that the best leaders always have a vision of where the organization is headed and why it matters, and they are good at communicating this vision to the people around them and throughout the company. Without vision, human institutions don't succeed.

"So, vision is a key part of leadership, something a leader must do, and something that makes a person a leader if he does it effectively."

"Exactly." Monte was warming to the topic. "I think initiative is another vital characteristic of leadership. As soon as a person takes on an effective initiative, he is leading. And if a leader doesn't ever take initiative, his leadership is stagnant. Thus in this project we are looking for people who have a vision of freedom and how truly free enterprise spreads opportunity to everyone in the society. We are also looking for people who know how to take initiative to improve things."

Nobody spoke for a few seconds, then Kami said, "It is interesting that the character traits essential to successful entrepreneurship are the same that are necessary for leadership in a free society." She paused to collect her thoughts, then continued, "For example, any kind of leader needs vision and the ability to articulate the vision, and that is true of every business leader both in entrepreneurial ventures and long-established companies.

"But where the manager of an older company may or may not need initiative, no entrepreneurial company can succeed without initiative-driven leaders."

"Actually," Monte said, "change is a constant, so initiative is essential in any company, new or old."

"That's been my experience, too," David affirmed. "Without initiative, no company keeps growing or succeeding. And the initiative must come from top leaders, or those leaders are eventually replaced."

"Okay," Kami said, "we've listed vision and initiative. What else makes a leader?"

"Initiative is essential," Monte said slowly, "but innovation is also needed to turn ideas into lasting systems, products, and services. And ingenuity is required to keep overcoming each new challenge. I know that initiative, innovation, and ingenuity seem similar, but they are actually different skills, and without all three no leader stays successful for long."

"The Three I's of Leadership?" Kami asked. "Is that a tag line for a marketing campaign to the 10 percent?"

"Add involvement, meaning political involvement, and make it the Four I's of Leadership," Marcus suggested.

"Would influence be better than involvement?" asked Amy.

"Maybe," Monte said, "but we need to get tenacity or persistence in there somewhere."

"And resiliency," Marcus added.

David found it difficult to follow the conversation, because something was nagging him. It was right there in the back of his mind, but he wasn't sure what it was. *Something about the way we are approaching leadership traits,* he thought.

It started when Kami was talking about the three branches of government, and then the three levels of government, and the nagging feeling just keeps growing. David had learned to listen when his intuition was trying to tell him something, so he suggested to the whole group, "Let's break for ninety minutes. For those of you here in the room, the area outside the hotel is beautiful, and it's a perfect time to find a quiet place alone and brainstorm ideas on leadership.

"For those of you at home, do the same. Let's all brainstorm, write down our thoughts, and meet again to discuss what we each come up with. Sometimes a meeting of the minds is best, and other times we all need to listen to our inner feelings and thoughts. What are our minds trying to tell us that isn't making it into the group discussion? Let's all do this small vision-quest exercise and then meet back here in ninety minutes to share our thoughts. Does this sound good?"

"Great," Monte said, as the others nodded.

Marcus was the first one out of the room.

12

"You all have your assignments," Josh announced. "Break into groups and help them remember. You've worked hard to inspire each person, and now is the time for them to recall the most important lessons."

David went directly to his room and grabbed his golf bag. Then he walked down to the clubhouse and got a bag of balls. As he sat on the bench near the practice greens and changed into his golf shoes, he mulled the ideas over in his mind. *It's something about putting three opposing forces into balance,* he told himself.

He walked to the driving range and began to mindlessly hit balls as far as he could. *What three leadership characteristics need to be balanced?*

After two slices in a row, David stopped swinging and stood looking far down the driving range. The warmth of the San Diego sun felt good, and it reminded him of the weather at home in Florida. He cleared his mind, pushed the tee into the ground, and hit the ball high and far.

He took a deep breath and hit another ball even farther than the last. He put his whole focus on the drives, and beads of sweat were forming on his brow by the time he finished the bucket.

David returned to the bench and sat down. He leaned back and looked at the gorgeous desert landscape that surrounded the golf course. He noticed Marcus sitting with his back to a tree near the clubhouse, writing in his notebook.

David pulled out his own small notepad and a pen. Many of his employees used laptops for this kind of notetaking, but he had learned that the movement of typing only uses dozens of movements while the natural motion of the fingers while writing things with a pen requires thousands of movements and causes deeper and more nuanced thinking—as well as better recall. Over time, he had noticed that the top leaders in most organizations wrote things out while many of their employees preferred typing.

The break from thinking about the freedom project had cleared his mind, and the physical movement of swinging the driver had relaxed him. "Time to focus," he said softly to himself.

He flipped open the front cover and wrote on the first page: "Leadership Traits of the 10 percent."

He read and reread the words on his page. He shook his head and crossed out what he had written. He turned the page and looked at the blank paper. *The Five Laws of Decline need to be the guiding focus. They always help me get past these roadblocks.* Then he wrote: "Sturgeon's Law and Leadership."

On the next line he continued: "What can Sturgeon's Law tell us about the most important leadership traits?"

The old feeling washed over him, and he smiled as he turned on his analytical mind. *About 10 percent of leaders will be great at vision, about 10 percent at initiative, and about 10 percent at tenacity.*

David put down his pen and shook his head again. *Something isn't right . . .*

Then it clicked. *That's the wrong way to look at it. We're considering traits, but leaders don't lead traits. They lead people. Or tasks and projects. Or, much of the time, themselves. Self-discipline is the first key to leadership, after all.* David tried to summon to his consciousness what he had read about these three legs of leadership in the book *Launching a Leadership Revolution.*

What makes someone a great leader? David had thought about this a lot over the years, and now he revisited the question with a focus on an American turnaround. *Greatness isn't a matter of one's character traits, but rather the result of choices.*

That's what made George Washington and Abraham Lincoln great. They faced overwhelming challenges, and they responded not so much by reacting but by leading—they saw where things needed to go, and they took action to sway the course of history.

They saw where the world was, and also where it needed to go, and then they put themselves between the two in a way that changed things toward the ideal.

It was often hard for them, but they did it anyway. And they looked beyond the common wisdom of their day and aimed for something better. Then they convinced the whole nation, and by extension the world, to go with them. The same can be said of many others, from Franklin and Madison to Andrew Carnegie and Margaret Thatcher.

David wrote these names on his notepad. *Some did it through their writing, and there are few words more powerful than Jefferson's "All men are created equal" or "When in the course of human events...." Or less-famous words like Richard Weaver's writings on "Ideas have consequences" or Bastiat's words in* The Law.

Some did it through their speeches, like Patrick Henry's "Give me liberty, or give me death," and Martin Luther King Jr.'s "I have a dream." Or the original Martin Luther's challenge to the panel of judges when he said, "Here I stand!" And Winston Churchill swayed the world when he announced that an "Iron Curtain" had descended over much of Europe.

Others invented or created, such as Thomas Edison, Albert Einstein, Beethoven, Shakespeare, or Picasso. Still others did it by example, like Joan of Arc, or Gandhi. In fact, example isn't just part of leadership—it's the most important part. Sam Walton, Walt Disney, Ray Kroc, Steve Jobs, and many other great business leaders have shown this repeatedly.

David lifted his pen and looked around at the beauty of the golf course. Again he noticed Marcus across the field, still writing feverishly. *The greatest changes came from teams of leaders, or groups of leaders working together. It is no accident that Socrates, Plato, Aristotle, and Alexander the Great were contemporaries. Without all four working in the same era, their ideas probably wouldn't have had such influence, and certainly would have had less impact if peppered across history.*

For example, Cicero lost to Caesar because he was basically alone as a great freedom thinker in his time. He needed someone like Washington or Confucius to partner with him.

And the Bible is so powerful in part because it is a collection of many writings from different leaders all sharing a connected, inspired message. When Jesus Christ wanted to change the world he called twelve leaders, trained them, and sent them out to alter the course of the whole world. It's like Margaret Mead said: "Never doubt that a small group of thoughtful, committed citizens can change the world. Indeed it is the only thing that ever has."

The American founding generation wouldn't have done much if Washington had been alone, but it is amazing how few top leaders there really were. Just a handful brought the big changes, including Washington, Franklin, the cousins Sam and John Adams, Jefferson, Madison, and Hamilton.

There are a few others who had a real impact, like John Hancock, Nathan Hale, George Mason, John Dickinson, Abigail Adams, Robert Morris, John Marshall, and James Wilson, but few Americans have ever even heard of the other Framers, like Oliver Ellsworth or Nathaniel Gorham.

A few committed, top leaders made all the difference. That's certainly always the case in successful businesses. And in a business turnaround, it is vital. The leadership team determines the future of any organization, and the success of a business or society never rises above the quality of its leadership.

David watched a group of three golfers tee off at the first hole, then he turned back to his notepad. "So much depends on leadership," he wrote. Then he said it again aloud. He glanced back through his notes, and he stopped on the idea that it's not a leader's talents, potential, or traits but rather his or her actions that make the difference. "Success is defined by the three legs of leadership," he read.

Suddenly David had a new thought, and he realized what had been nagging him. "That's it!" he said out loud. He grinned widely and pulled a red pen from his jacket. He had learned that when a eureka moment comes, it is important to write it all down as quickly as possible, before the energy of the epiphany dissipates.

David flipped to a new page and began to write:

"The three legs of leadership are character, tasks, and relationships. True leaders must lead their own character, they must effectively lead tasks and projects, and they must be excellent in leading other people. And it goes even deeper than this."

He quickly wrote the main idea:

"Based on Sturgeon's Law, in an organization 10 percent of the leaders will have great leadership character, another 10 percent will have great task-oriented leadership, and another 10 percent will be great relationship leaders.

"Combine these segments together, and guess what? About 10 percent of these leaders will have *all* of these traits, or about one leader in a thousand people. Those are our top leaders."

David sat back and sighed with relief. *This is big. This is huge, in fact. Sturgeon's Law predicts our current national decline, but it also provides the solutions.*

He repeated the breakthrough in his mind: *According to Sturgeon's Law, about 10 percent of effective leaders are really good at all three types of leadership, and these are the top leaders. In fact, they are capable of being influential leaders like the great men and women from history. This is the crux of leadership!*

David wrote: "Indeed, these are the leaders of the needed

American turnaround. If they do their part, the future of freedom and prosperity will be bright. If not, there will be no turnaround. It is that simple.

"Think of the Five Laws of Decline as the X axis," he wrote, "and character, tasks, and relationships as the Y axis. Then consider each of the Five Laws as they relate to character leadership. When you are done with this, do the same for task leadership. And finally look at all Five Laws of Decline in terms of relationship leadership. This X/Y axis comparison allows us to break down a person's leadership and see exactly what to focus on. Furthermore, it..."

David smiled as he imagined hearing Amy's voice in his mind: *No math. Just explain it as simply as possible.* He chuckled to himself and crossed out the X and Y graph. "When you're right, you're right, Amy," he said softly.

David was in the flow now, and he kept writing:

"The Five Laws of Decline tell us what is really causing the problem and how to fix it, which in this case is a lack of leadership by the 10 percent who should be closely watching our government and keeping it in its place—both by their leadership and by inspiring the rest of the citizens to take the right actions to protect freedom."

David went back and read what he'd written, then he stood and pumped his fist like he had just hit a hole-in-one. *I'm on a golf course, so why not?* He felt like a huge weight had been removed from his shoulders.

David called Monte on his iPhone and read all his notes aloud to him.

"What do you think?" David asked.

"It's what Jefferson called a natural aristocracy," Monte said. "And this fixes the whole project. We don't have to try to reach millions and millions of people. We just need to reach the top leaders, who according to Sturgeon's Law will be found in all states and regions. We need them to start putting their leadership skills toward overseeing the government and promoting freedom."

"Exactly." David was excited that Monte agreed with him about the importance of this development. "It is more manageable, and more realistic."

Monte responded, "Yes. This tells us which citizens are naturally part of the 10 percent. So, put the two models together, Sturgeon's Law on the one hand and the three legs of leadership on the other, and we know what the problem is and who needs to solve it.

"In short, we're looking for those with high levels of leadership in character, tasks, and relationships—all three—which narrows things down a lot."

David was passionate now, and he put down his pen as he talked. "We can do this! That's our scoreboard. That's what we're looking for."

"And there'll be such a person for about every thousand people in the country," Monte said enthusiastically. "This is a real breakthrough."

13

"They're making fabulous progress, Mr. President. You might want to get over there just in case."

"Good idea, Josh. I'll stay close as long as they're meeting."

David's energy was infectious as he shared what he had experienced during the vision-quest exercise, and the whole group unconsciously leaned forward.

Everyone considered David's words. After a few seconds, Kami asked, "So, in a nation of about 200 million available adults, we are really looking for around two hundred thousand leaders who meet the three criteria at extremely high levels, right? And they're already naturally spread around the nation."

"According to Sturgeon's Law, yes," David said.

"Plus the other leadership groups we talked about earlier," Monte added. "They're all important. At some point, we need to talk more about that group of Jeffersons, the ones who know the freedom principles in serious depth."

"I reviewed John Naisbitt's writings about the megatrends of our times," Marcus said, "and I made a lot of notes about the importance of keeping high-touch, personalized solutions combined with high-tech influences.

"We want to lead both people and tasks, to put it in David's terms. I think if we're low-tech or low-touch we'll fail in this endeavor, but a high-tech and high-touch strategy fits right in with finding leaders who are excellent at character, tasks, and relationships at the same time."

David nodded. "And this answers our concerns earlier today about the actual numbers," he said.

"It also ties to the American Founders in a...truly...remarkable...way." Kami pronounced each word with emphasis. Then she shook her head in amazement.

Everyone was looking at her, so she continued. "Well, several of the Founders said they got many of their most important ideas on government from the Bible, but modern scholars have often disagreed with this view, showing that they got the three branches of government along with separations of power and so on from writers like Polybius, David Hume, and Montesquieu.

"But according to modern computer studies of the founding writings, the Founders quoted the Bible more than any other book, and the most frequently quoted part of the Bible was Deuteronomy, especially chapter one. You can read the studies of founding writings by Donald Lutz and Charles Hyneman to learn more about this and to study the other things the Founders read and quoted. It's really very fascinating.

"In fact, the constitutions of colonial Connecticut and Rhode Island were based on this chapter, and after the U.S. Constitution was adopted these were the only two states that didn't have to alter their constitutions to work under the new system.

"Anyway, Deuteronomy chapter one taught the ancient Israelites to set up their whole political system based on local political groupings of 10 families, 50 families, 100 families, and finally 1,000 families.

"The elected heads of each group were known as judges of 10, judges of 50, and so on, and during times of war they were also called captains of 10, 50, 100, etc. The era described in the Book of Judges was run under this political system.

"But here's the main thing: the person elected head of the one thousand was the top leader in local politics, and the people were basically encouraged to elect these leaders of the thousand based on their character, ability to lead in tasks and projects, and effectiveness in relationships. I mean, it isn't spelled out in exactly these words, but the similarities are striking."

Kami continued. "The Anglo-Saxons adopted this same model, and their traditions helped lead to the Magna Carta and several other eras of English freedom over the centuries.

"It's just incredible that the American Founders saw this and built towns and counties on this model, and that now this group is coming to the same conclusion from business models without any knowledge of this biblical, Anglo-Saxon background and the history of American townships during the colonial era.

"Or"—Kami looked at David—"did you already know this?"

He shook his head.

"Weird," Marcus said.

"I think this is an important discussion we're having," Michelle said, just loud enough for everyone to hear.

Marcus hated it when business meetings turned to what he called "the touchy-feely stuff," but he knew what to do in such situations. "I think you all owe me an apology," he announced loudly. "If I hadn't been talking about the balance of the three levels of luxury watches, Kami and David wouldn't have come up with any of this today."

Everyone laughed.

"I think that's a stretch," Kami said, still laughing.

"And I think we should break for the afternoon," Marcus said, looking deliberately at his watch in a way that everyone could see how expensive it was.

The whole group burst into even louder laughter.

"Okay, everyone, when they meet in the morning, I want everyone to be at their best.

"Figure out what each participant needs to remember, or feel, and get them ready through the night. Dreams are one of our best tools.

"You all know what to do, right?"

"Yes, Mr. President," everyone said in unison.

W elcome," David said. "How did everyone sleep?"

After nods and positive words from everyone, David summarized the goals for the day. "We made a lot of progress yesterday, and by the end of today we want to have a truly workable scoreboard for the leaders of an American turnaround.

"I made a few more notes last night about the three legs of leadership, and I think we should start there."

After ensuring that everyone was enthusiastically engaged, David began. "First of all, as Michael Gerber taught in *The E-Myth*, people want to work with a motivating leader, but they also want to work in an environment where leaders have created a clearly defined structure for success in the organization's endeavors. They want to feel that the work they do is truly worth doing.

"Furthermore, great companies know how to help their employees work at the intersection of passion ('What are we passionate about?'), potential ('What can we be the best at?'), and profits ('What drives our economic engine?').

"In nonprofit organizations, the intersection is passion, potential, and purpose (or mission). For America, the underpinning purpose has always been freedom and the opportunities that flow from freedom, what the Founders called life, liberty, and the pursuit of happiness.

"So, the clearly defined structure for success is what we've long called the American Dream, and it consists of the intersection of our national passion, our potential, and our freedoms."

Kami spoke up. "Another way to say this, in more political terms, is that our best future will be found at the intersection of our dreams and goals as free people, the level of our economic opportunities, and the quality of our freedoms."

"Exactly." David nodded. "The three legs of leadership measure each of the three leadership criteria—leadership of character, task, and relationships—on a scale of 1 to 10, then multiplies each of these together for a final score. For example, if someone rated themselves a two on Character, three on Task, and two on Relationships, their score would be $2 \times 3 \times 2 = 12$. The lowest possible score would be 0, and the highest score would be $10 \times 10 \times 10 = 1,000$."

"Too much math," Amy warned with a smile.

"I'm almost done with the math," David said, "but this is important. Just give me one more minute.

"Note that Sturgeon's Law is really a positive for leaders, because it says that all of us can become effective leaders if we are willing to work at it.

"Kami's discussion of Deuteronomy yesterday reminded me that the one-in-a-thousand ratio is discussed by many leadership gurus around the world. For example, Malcolm Gladwell reported that a performer can build and maintain a community of around 100 to 150 people, but a real leader, one who leads performers of several such groups, develops about once in a thousand people.

"If one is building a community or group of thousands of people, then top leaders are required, leaders who break through Sturgeon's Law on all three legs of leadership: character, tasks, and relationships."

"So, we're looking for people who are already leading over one thousand people on a regular, ongoing basis," Monte said.

"And such leaders aren't going to just follow us or anyone else," Marcus said.

"Right," Monte affirmed. "Leaders of this magnitude refuse to work for time punchers, dictators, or micromanagers, but they love responsibility and visionary leadership." Kami was shaking her head, so Monte stopped.

"What are you thinking, Kami?" David asked.

"Two things," she answered. "First, the only way to reach such leaders is to attract them. There is really no other way to get them involved. So, like we said yesterday, our scoreboard for an American turnaround has to be something that attracts top leaders and makes them *want* to take part. Most of them aren't joiners, so they have to buy into something they really care about."

David nodded. "I agree. True servant leadership, as taught by Robert Greenleaf, Ken Blanchard, and others, means being the kind of leader who attracts other top leaders into one's community, thus creating a team of leaders who drive change in any field they set their minds to."

"Yes, but that's only half of it."

The rest of the group looked at Kami in surprise.

15

James and Josh exchanged a look.

"They might just do it, Mr. President."

"Yes, they might. I should get down there, like yesterday. This whole thing could be swayed in so many directions."

"Mr. President, are you sure this is a good idea?"

James considered. "I'm not sure ... but I'll be smart."

After a few more seconds, he added, "And careful."

W hat do you mean?" Marcus asked Kami.

"Well, what David said is right on. One of the best books on servant leadership is *Leadership and Self-Deception* by the Arbinger Institute, and it teaches exactly what David just said. Has anyone read it?"

When everyone nodded, Kami smiled. "I really love discussing things with this group! You have read all the same books, and that makes meaningful conversation easy. Anyway, the first half of top leadership is being the kind of leader who attracts other top leaders into one's team, as David already said.

"The other half is finding ways to work with, partner with, and cooperate with other top leaders who have their own communities. It can't all be about one organization, no matter how great it is. In fact, the better an organization is, the more top leaders it has, and

the more it needs to be able to work with other top leaders and organizations in order to make a real difference in society.

"Throughout history, organizations that try to change everything alone are always more limited than organizations with the
same quality of leadership that find ways to partner with other top
groups."

"Absolutely," David and Monte said at the same time.

David could see that the normal morning lull was wearing off
and people were really investing in the conversation. "What's the
second thing you wanted to mention, Kami?"

"Well, I hesitate to bring this up, but I think we need to be clear
that in any serious national shift we're going to have two big factions competing with each other. The 10 percent will change things,
but we're going to have to deal with the fact that about half of the
top leaders are going to disagree on some major points.

"I don't know if that happens in business turnarounds. I mean,
if they disagree with the leadership on fundamental points, I assume
you don't put them in top leadership roles. Or maybe you do. Sam
Walton taught that such diversity was essential. But in a nation,
you're always going to have the Whigs and the Tories, the Loyal-
ists and the Patriots, the Federalists and the Anti-Federalists, the
Republicans and the Democrats, or some other adversarial pairing.

"It just works that way. The 10 percent are going to be divided
into two major groups, and probably a few minor groups. Is that a
problem?"

"Actually," David said, "my first thought when I woke up this
morning was about the Anti-Federalists. I just couldn't get it out
of my mind how many things they got right. In fact, most of the
major challenges we are now facing in this nation—the very things
that have made it so we need a turnaround—were predicted by the
Anti-Federalists."

David stopped, but everyone just looked at him, so he kept

talking. "My point is that we needed the Federalists. Without them we wouldn't have had a Constitution at all. But we also needed the Anti-Federalists. I know this sounds crazy, but I wish we had two groups of leaders in today's world who knew as much about the principles and details of freedom as the Federalists and Anti-Federalists.

"They thought they were enemies, but from the perspective of our day, they were both necessary to the establishment of American freedom."

"So," Amy said, "what you're saying is that we just need to help the 10 percent get truly involved, and then to trust that their arguments will work to the nation's benefit, even if we end up disagreeing with some of their decisions?"

"Yes," chimed in Kami. "I know you were asking David, but the answer has to be yes. Otherwise the turnaround won't work. It has to be built on many top leaders, not just on the ones we like the most. In fact, the more top leaders we get from different groups around the nation, with differing views, the more likely this will really work. The key is that, whatever their views, they are top leaders and they understand the principles of freedom in real depth—like the American Founders did."

"I agree," David said. "But that isn't our big challenge right now. Of course top leaders will have intense discussions and even disagreements, but that's what freedom and leadership require. We have such divisions right now in the current political parties, but they don't always take America in the right direction.

"I think the big problem is that the 10 percent isn't doing its role in helping the regular people have a real say in leading America. So, for the most part we're left with only political leaders, not leaders from all parts of American life. That's what we have to change."

"The three legs of leadership will work," Kami said confidently. "If we can get the top leaders in the nation, from all walks of life, really focused on an American turnaround and discussing it with each other and with an eye toward application, we'll see real change."

David realized that Michelle was being very quiet again today. "What are your thoughts on all this, Michelle?" he asked.

She let out a long sigh. "Are you sure you want to know?"

Everyone nodded, so Michelle sat forward and took a deep breath. "Here goes," she said. "Truthfully, I'm thinking that many of these top leaders aren't really focused on politics. We have a lot of political officials, and probably a bunch of them are top leaders. But it seems that as a nation we've decided to leave politics, freedom, and even economics to the experts—or those who pass as experts.

"So my big concern is how we can get the nonpolitical leaders to get actively involved in political issues. They're so busy building their businesses, or leading their religious congregations if they're ministers, or teaching, coaching, training young people in music or theater, running their law or accounting or engineering firms, or whatever they do for a living. Not to mention their favorite entertainments, whether it is sports, movies, vacations, or whatever.

"And I think a lot of the top leaders are mothers who are focused on raising their children. They may not be leading a thousand people, but the depth of how they influence their children is worth leading thousands."

She paused and shook her head. "In short, I think most of these nonpolitical leaders care deeply about freedom and America, but we've been taught to elect the right officials and hope that our president, senator, congressman, or governor fixes things for us.

"You're all talking about getting regular citizens to turn a lot of their attention from their businesses, families, and lives to leading our nation, and I just can't help but feel that this is going to be more difficult than you think. You are used to working in business, where a person's job is to get excited about your scoreboards and performance. But this is a whole different thing."

Michelle stopped talking, and the members of the meeting sat pondering in silence.

16

"The Anti-Federalists? Really, James?"

"Uh...yes, sir. One of our team thought it would help, and he impressed it on David in the night. I was as surprised as you. But maybe, just maybe, it's exactly what is needed. I respect my team, sir, and if it turns out to be wrong I take full responsibility."

"That's surprising, coming from you. I thought that whole Federalist debate was over."

"Well, sir, if we're going to have to fix things in our day as well as David's, maybe it's time to revisit it all."

The man took off his spectacles and gave James a long, searching look.

The solution, I think, is to find a way to tie the political system with the economic system," David told the group. "Michelle is right. As long as people have to divide their lives between the needs and wants of their families and careers, they're not going to have much time left over for political influence.

"I know the Founders wanted to leave economics alone, because they thought if every person was treated equally before the law the aristocratic class system would disappear and free enterprise would flourish. In truth, this worked very well for a long time. But eventually the government got bigger and bigger, and the Law of Diminishing Returns kicked in.

"The Constitution was the best thing the Founders could come up with. And while it had some major flaws, especially in regard to slavery, it allowed a lot of freedom, and over time the people used their freedom to improve the whole nation. They even eventually got rid of slavery, though I think they should have done it much sooner.

"But think about it—what caused this great Constitution and the freedoms it established to decline? Why have we lost so many freedoms over the course of American history?"

David could see that not everybody was getting his point, so he turned to Kami. "What would you say are the major causes contributing to the loss of American freedoms?"

"Well," Kami said, "I should start by saying that I think there was an element of inspiration in the founding of the Constitution. It wasn't just brilliance. I believe it was, as they put it in the *Federalist Papers*, helped by the hand of Providence. But to answer your question, the Constitution faced elements of decline right from the beginning.

"Don't get me wrong, however. The Constitution certainly did have flaws, especially slavery, like David said. Over time American freedom spread and eventually corrected most of the flaws. For example, the Civil War ended slavery, women got more rights through lots of work and effort, and during the civil rights movement more inalienable rights were passed on to all citizens. Freedom works, and a free society tends to increase in freedom as long as it values liberty.

"But on the negative side, without going into a lot of detail, a number of Supreme Court cases between 1803 and 1824 decreased the power of the states and, by extension, the freedom of the people. This continued through the Civil War era and into the early 1900s.

"Then in 1913 we saw the creation of the Federal Reserve, the income tax amendment, and the loss of state power when the Seventeenth Amendment stopped state legislatures from electing senators. All of these reduced the power of the states and the people and shifted a lot of the power to Washington, D.C.

"In 1936, the Supreme Court found in the famous *United States v. Butler* case that the federal government could do whatever it considered good for the nation, without being limited by the Constitution. The details are a little more complex than that, but that's the crux of what happened.

"After that, government has grown by leaps and bounds under nearly every presidential administration, regardless of which political party was in power. And as government has grown, the costs have risen and the people have been required to foot the bill. Even more important, our own freedoms have, for the most part, decreased in direct relation to the growth of the federal government.

"Another source of decline has come from the treaty power in the Constitution, which has allowed the government to change laws and policies by ratifying treaties rather than getting the regular votes from both houses of Congress.

"Also, we could talk about the problems caused by executive orders and the way the executive branch has overstepped its powers.

"Together, these are the big ways our freedoms and the constitutional form of our government have eroded. Does that answer your question, or do you want me to go into more depth?"

"That's fine for now," David said. "But I have one big question: Why? Why were all these things allowed to happen?"

"Well," Kami answered, "starting at the beginning, Jefferson saw what the Court was doing in 1803 and argued that—"

"Yes," he interrupted, "Jefferson and John Marshall argued about the role of the Court, and in the Civil War era various leaders debated the pros and cons of increased power in Washington. Later, various national leaders debated the changes of 1913, as well as the *Butler* case and so many other cases, not to mention the various changes in our laws created by executive orders or treaties like the Bretton Woods Agreement of 1944 or the proposed Rome Statute of 1998.

"But why did all of these happen? Why did the Constitution break down? What was supposed to stop these kinds of things from occurring?"

"I see what you mean," Kami said. "In all of these situations, freedom was ultimately lost for the same reason. The people let it happen. The Constitution gave them power to stop these things, but they didn't use it. They assumed their political leaders would do it for them. They were focused on other things, like making a living and raising their families, and they just let their freedoms be written away."

"How could they have changed these outcomes?" David asked.

"Easy. They could have voted differently. Or let their leaders know how strongly they felt on certain government actions."

"Well, why didn't they? I mean, you said they were focused on other things, but if they had been focusing on keeping their freedoms, what would they have done differently? Or, more to the point, did they even know they were losing their freedoms?"

"No, most people didn't know their freedoms were in jeopardy. Few people read Supreme Court cases, or treaties, or proposed laws—"

"Just like today," David said.

He looked around the room, and at the screen, making eye contact with each participant. "As we discussed earlier," he said slowly, "a key part of leadership is doing the tasks of leaders. Peter Drucker says this is *the* vital part of leadership. And one essential task of a free people is to closely study everything government is doing and keep it always within its constitutional limits.

"When the people stop doing this, in any free nation, freedom begins to erode."

17

Josh and his team were so focused on the meeting that they didn't notice when the tall man entered. When Josh saw him, he immediately stood.

The rest of the team noticed, saw the man, and stood in respect.

"That's not necessary," the man said, and waved them back to their seats. "Where is James?"

"He went down, sir. Just in case he was needed."

"Ah..."

David turned to Kami again. "But at some point the people do get involved, stand up, try to take back control of their government. So what causes this change in their behavior?"

"It is nearly always the result of a major crisis of some kind," she said. "When they feel threatened or that their livelihoods or families are in danger, they get involved."

"I think all of this helps us in our search for the 10 percent, and also for how to reach them," David said, as he scanned the group. "In the founding era, an interesting thing happened that is very different from today. In our time, the political leaders, the societal influencers—like scholars, journalists, entertainers, writers, religious leaders, and others—and the business leaders are three separate groups.

"But in the founding era they all came together to promote

freedom. They all felt the keen lack of economic and political freedoms, and they all got involved. As Kami told us yesterday, only about 3 percent actually made things happen, but this group included top leaders from all four sectors of society—not just the political leaders."

"Wait," Monte interrupted. "You said 'four sectors,' but you only listed three—political leaders, influencers, and business leaders. What's the fourth?"

"As Michelle told us earlier, the fathers and mothers are a vital source and key component of all top leaders. I'm convinced that top parents are part of this equation. Just look at the influence of Abigail Adams, for example."

"You could list them as part of the influencers," Marcus suggested.

"Either way, they need to be included in the plan, because they make all the difference," Amy said.

"We need to get all four actively involved in the American turnaround," David told the group. "In fact, there's a special word for a society where the four groups don't really work together on big things, where the political leaders make the governmental decisions while the business leaders focus on profit and growth, and families and influencers are content not to be involved in governance. And that word is *decline*.

"But there's also a word for those societies where top leaders from all the groups work together to govern the nation, and it's a word we've almost lost in our current world: *community*. That's what a community is—a place where the leaders of all parts of society work together to govern it."

David quit speaking and let his words sink in.

"I think I disagree," a voice said.

Surprised, everyone turned to look at the small man standing in the doorway.

David immediately recognized him as the gentleman who sat next to him on his flight, and he struggled to recall his name.

"I'm James," the man said, "and I couldn't help overhearing you from the hallway. I'm waiting for a meeting in the next conference room, but your conversation for the past few minutes is so interesting I just had to share one thought.

"I know this is probably in very poor manners," he said to the gathering, "but David and I talked for hours on the airplane a few days ago, and when I heard his voice I was surprised and stopped to listen.

"In any case, I just want to say one thing and then I'll leave. I think the influencers and the parents are already deeply concerned about America, and they are ready to engage the turnaround if they only knew what to do. As for the political class, its members are deeply involved but too often swayed—either by professional advancement or partisan attachments—to lead in new directions. New thinking is needed.

"Tocqueville noted in the 1830s that as go the attorneys, so goes the United States. But today this rule has changed. As go the business leaders, so goes America. I know that many business leaders are deeply concerned about current trends, especially the growing inefficiencies in Washington, but few are fully engaged in actively bringing about a lasting change.

"If you get the business leaders to take action in turning around this nation, it will happen. The other sectors will follow them, and they can provide new thinking and directions that the politicians are too entrenched to engage.

"The parents and influencers will take part naturally when the business leaders lead out. Again, as go the business leaders, so goes America. That's your key to making this work. "

The man turned and left as quickly as he had come.

Surprised once again, David stood and rapidly walked to the door to ask for the man's business card, but when he reached the hallway James was already gone.

"That was strange," Amy said.

"I thought he was pretty cool," Marcus said. "I loved his pocket watch. It's clearly quality, but I have no idea what brand it is."

"Do you think he's right?" Michelle asked.

"I do," Monte said immediately.

"Me, too," Kami agreed.

After a long pause, David decided it was time for a break. "I do, too," he told the group. "And I think we've got to find a way to get business leaders to see the direct value of becoming passionately involved citizens."

PART II

18

"Well, yes, sir ... it may have been a little bold to just go and talk to them. But it helped them decide to do the special retreat and invite the additional people. My team has been working very hard to encourage them to get the right people involved. This next meeting should help our project immensely."

"I see. Do you expect any more direct meetings?"

"I don't know. But if they are needed, I'll do it again. Do you see any problem with that?"

"No ... Be wise about it, James." Then, after a long pause, the taller man turned to face his protégé. "James," he said, "I'm starting to think it's going to work this time."

"I agree." James nodded. Then, more cautiously, he said, "Maybe it will."

There are at least three issues with your plan," Wendell said, as David steered the car into the parking lot of the golf course.

"Kami said the trail head is just behind the clubhouse," David said. "Let's talk as we hike."

The two men got their small packs from the trunk and headed up the trail toward the Park City peak. They walked briskly at first, and nobody spoke.

After a few minutes, they reached the second switchback in the trail and naturally slowed down when a break in the trees provided a beautiful view of the golf course stretching below them in the foothills.

Wendell put one foot on a fence railing, and the two caught their breath as they admired the view. "Let's walk more slowly and talk," David suggested, as both men turned back up the trail.

It was barely 6 a.m., and the cool mountain morning energized the hikers. The smell of pines and the quaking leaves of the aspens surrounded them with a sense of possibility. After a few steps, David asked, "So, you were saying that there are three problems?"

"Not *problems*," Wendell said, smiling, "just issues. They'll only become problems if we don't address them right from the beginning."

"I like how you think," David said. He loved the mountain views, the smell of the forest, the tall trees. For some reason, he felt a natural rapport with Wendell, even though he had only talked to him by phone and e-mail before this morning. "So, what are they?"

Wendell continued: "I agree with you that business leaders are the future of America. Of course, they aren't the only leaders, but without them the whole project will struggle to succeed. That said, I think we need to more clearly understand what we actually mean by business leaders."

The trail went through a clearing made for the ski lifts, and the two men watched the empty lift chairs pass by as they crossed toward the forest on the other side.

"This is the first issue. Put simply, there is a significant difference between business leaders with an entrepreneurial mind-set and those who see the world as a climb up the corporate ladder. I call them the Creators and the Credentialists, and their worldviews are entirely different.

"The Credentialists care about, well, themselves. They want to get promoted and obtain all the perks that go with business success. They are leaders, yes, but leadership is often simply a means to an end for them. Success and achievement are their goals, and leadership is only a vehicle toward their objectives.

"Creators, in contrast, see things from the exact opposite view. They see leadership as the true goal, improving the world as the objective, and success, achievement, promotion, and other aspects of business as the real means to their vision of a better world."

Wendell glanced at David to see if he agreed or had concerns, but David was nodding in agreement as they walked, so he continued. "Of course, it's not really that cut and dried. Everyone is a little bit Creator and also part Credentialist, but most people ultimately fit into one camp or the other.

"And those who care mostly about climbing the corporate ladder are always going to put themselves first. Of course, what we really want are Creators—business leaders who will put freedom and leadership first. This really matters."

"I agree," David said. "It reminds me of the whole concept of servant leadership. For example, John Maxwell teaches in *The 21 Irrefutable Laws of Leadership* that leaders add value to the exact extent that they truly serve others."

"Right." Wendell slowed his walking slightly in order to talk more. "That's Maxwell's Law 5, what he calls the Law of Addition. We add exactly what we serve. Service is the whole thing.

"Also," Wendell continued, "in that same book he teaches Law 10, the Law of Connection. In short, that law says that leaders must touch hearts before they ask people to do things."

"Heart first, then hands," David summarized.

They both smiled. They had spent breakfast sharing favorite books and being amazed at how many readings and ideas they had in common.

"Yes. And the best way to touch hearts is to serve. So that's the first issue. We need to reach Creators, not just Credentialists. The Credentialists won't stick with leading society. They'll eventually drop the freedom project and just focus back on themselves."

The two men continued to hike, and then David asked, "What's the second concern?"

"Well, before we go there, let me say one more thing about attracting these entrepreneurial types, rather than only Credentialists. Creators succeed only if they partner with Builders. The Builders are those who aren't always creating something new but who do much of the heavy lifting to turn innovation into lasting organizations. Together, Creators and Builders are the real entrepreneurial-minded leaders.

"Creators innovate things, and without them new things wouldn't get started. Then Builders come along and turn great ideas and foundations into lasting institutions. It's a true partnership, and both Creators and Builders need each other.

"The Credentialists, in contrast, tend to partner with the Bureaucrats, those who use position and rules to manage things. The bureaucratic-minded care mostly about protecting the benefits they have, keeping things from changing, and avoiding risk.

"Together, the Credentialists and Bureaucrats seek to stop innovation. The Bureaucrats are resistant to change, and the Credentialists want everything to remain the same except with them in higher positions of authority. If society changes too much, the Credentialists' plans for promotion will lose their importance.

"For example, Socrates brought a whole new level of thinking to Athens, but he was shut down by the bureaucratic-minded parts of his society and the Credentialists in those days who wanted things to remain unaltered. This pattern has repeated itself many times in history, from the story of Moses and Pharaoh's court to the American Founders versus the British Parliament.

"Basically, Credentialists and Bureaucrats cooperate to fight the innovation of Creators and Builders."

After they walked for a long time, David stopped and sat on a large rock. "I'm so glad Kami suggested this retreat," he said, as Wendell drank from his water bottle. "At first, I wasn't sure it would be worth the expense, but this conversation has already justified the whole thing."

"Yes, Kami is brilliant." Wendell took another drink. "When she first asked me to mentor her, I gave her an impossible project and thought that was the end of her. I told her to get a $30,000 donation to help a school we support in Madagascar. When she came back six weeks later with several checks in hand, I knew she was someone I wanted to work with. She's never disappointed me since."

"Actually, I wanted to ask you something about Kami," David said. "When I first met her, she was one of the most promising leaders in a company we were turning around, but she purposely ignored our normal performance criteria. When we asked her about it, she said she was testing us, which quite frankly surprised us. I'm still not sure what to think of it."

Wendell smiled widely. "Credible Dissonance," he said.

19

"I trust you, James. I just want to understand. Why do you need a full second team?"

"The first team is stretched too thin already, sir."

"I know David has expanded the project, but do you really need a second team?"

"Oh, the second team isn't for the David project. Not at all. I want the second team—call them Group 2—to go back in time and watch the American founding. I know I was assigned to encourage the FreedomShift in modern times, but I just keep thinking that the best way to do this is to study how we might have done things differently in the 1780s. I know it's unorthodox; but I want Group 2 to research this."

James paused, then added, "And, yes, I may intervene there, too, if needed."

What's Credible Dissonance?"

"Well, we live in a society that gives a lot of emphasis to credibility. Some would say *too* much. Societies that are run mostly by Credentialists and Bureaucrats have this problem. Think about it. If you're a Credentialist, your whole life is about getting ahead, getting good grades as a student, doing better on the SAT, getting into the best colleges, having the most prestigious credentials, the best jobs with prominent companies, the biggest house, and, above all, a highly esteemed title.

"Or, alternatively, you work from behind the scenes and define success by the status of the people you rub shoulders with.

"I'm not saying any of these things are bad, per se, but they can be taken too far. Credentials can be positive motivation for many things in life, but they can also become overly important in society.

"For example, if you're bureaucratic-minded, you want a set list of rules for what credentials are required for each job, each position, and you quickly become very uncomfortable if anyone ever works outside these clear and 'accepted' guidelines. In short, Credentialists and Bureaucrats love résumé credentials to an extreme level."

"But don't we all want to know who we're dealing with?" David asked.

"Yes, but there is another way. When you do a business turn-around, do you choose your leaders by their credentials, or by their performance?"

"Well, both. But ultimately, performance wins out. Credentials only matter in the long term to the extent that the leader might need to impress someone."

"Right," Wendell said. "Let's consider a concrete example. The American Founders cared about reason and performance much more than credentials. The British Parliament couldn't understand how the colonists could see things this way. Of course, by that point Britain was run mostly by Credentialists and Bureaucrats.

"The American Founders believed that all men are created equal, and that the logic of this statement spoke for itself. It was self-evident, they said. End of debate.

"But the British leaders just couldn't get past *who* wrote it. If it had been written by Edmund Burke or Lord Pitt, they would have given it serious consideration. But in their eyes it had been thrown together by a bunch of unknown, uncredentialed, and therefore 'unworthy' radicals in some hole-in-the-wall place across the ocean.

"If the experts at Oxford and Cambridge had been consulted, Parliament would have at least listened. But in the eyes of British leaders, our Founders were merely hicks in the woods."

"What Malcolm Gladwell calls Outliers," David said, "people from outside the expected areas of credentialed expertise who actually bring about most serious innovations."

"Exactly," responded Wendell. "One of the most important articles ever written in *Harvard Business Review* talked about Disruptive Innovations, where products and services, or even ideas, appear in unexpected places at the bottom of the market and then rise in influence until they displace the established institutions and competitors."

"Yes. I loved Clayton Christensen's book *The Innovator's Dilemma*," David said. "Innovation usually comes from outliers, like Steve Jobs and Bill Gates. And the American Founding Fathers are a great example of how this works."

Wendell whittled on a stick as he spoke. "For outliers—or as we call them, entrepreneurially minded leaders—credentials are irrelevant. Performance is all that matters. They care about results. In fact, performance and results *are* the credentials they respect."

"It makes sense," David said. "After all, out on the frontier, credentials weren't nearly as valuable as performance."

Wendell stood and stretched. "For example, when a prominent European naturalist wrote that the American deer was small in comparison to the British deer, and that this was indicative of the lesser intelligence of the American people, the upper classes of Europe took it as truth. Nothing the American scientists said was considered credible, because the Americans didn't have the credentials Europeans respected.

"Finally, in frustration, Thomas Jefferson purchased a set of elk antlers from the American plains and had them shipped across the Atlantic to the home of the famous scholar. But still, even after such indisputable proof of the size of deer species in the Americas, the scholar's credentials won the debate, and European naturalists still believed the credentialed side of the argument for many years."

"That's fascinating," David said. "Where can I read more about that?"

"Well, the naturalist was the Comte de Buffon, and I've read about it in a number books. Probably the most obvious one is the *Collected Writings of Thomas Jefferson*, but it's also on the Monticello .org website and shouldn't be hard to find online."

"That's so interesting," David mused. "The truth and the evidence don't always matter in the face of prestigious credentials."

"That's how Credible Dissonance works. And this fits right into our current conversation, because nearly all business leaders engage in Credible Dissonance quite frequently. In fact, that's my second concern.

"But first, back to Kami. She learned all about Credible Dissonance during the years I mentored her, and so she merely tested you when you came in and pushed to change the corporation where she worked. You probably expected to deal with Credentialists and Bureaucrats, and a few Creators and Builders, and you knew what to do with them. But Kami must have been a surprise. She's a Builder, maybe even a Creator, who acted like a Bureaucrat—but clearly wasn't."

"It was a bit of a shock, I'll admit. My friend Marcus had no idea how to read her."

"People who understand Credible Dissonance tend to be surprising, mainly because we don't expect it. But it's all around us. For example, I remember reading in a magazine article many years ago about this concept. They used a different name for Credible Dissonance, but I prefer this label because it so clearly identifies the problem.

"Anyway, I don't remember the article in detail, but one thing stood out. Imagine that you are a reporter, or a top aide for a New York state senator. You attend a political fund-raising banquet and find yourself sitting next to a self-made multimillionaire who built a dry-cleaning business from the ground up. The millionaire is credible because of his performance, and you owe your credibility mainly to your title."

"But you might be an excellent reporter," David countered.

"Yes," Wendell said, "but let's say the millionaire looks at you without recognizing your name. If you follow up by introducing yourself as Steven Morris, *New York Times*, he'll nod with recognition.

"But then, say he just introduces himself as Tom Whittaker. You feel pretty good about yourself because you have credibility by association due to the company you work for. After all, organizations like the *New York Times*, CNN, Standard Oil Company, or Yale University are known. He is just a guy named Tom.

"Then you scan the program for tonight's event and note Tom Whittaker as one of three platinum donors. Your newspaper paid the $5,000 per plate for you to attend, or they paid nothing and got you in with a press pass, but the man paid for himself and his five friends out of his own pocket, then donated another $275,000 to help elect tonight's main speaker. Your status, and possibly your credibility, immediately sinks in comparison.

"Still, you assure yourself, the *Times* is a national fixture, and who ever heard of his chain of dry-cleaning shops? The Credible Dissonance here is real. Yours comes from your employer. But are you, just you, Steven Morris, actually seen as credible? If you are a Credentialist or Bureaucrat, this matters. If you are a Creator or Builder, you couldn't care less.

"Then Tom begins to discuss politics with you. He has strong opinions, and he gets some of his facts wrong. You work in this kind of political debate every day, and you've learned how to pounce on misstated facts, but do you want to start an argument? You hesitate, and he keeps talking.

"The more opinionated he is, the more he slants the facts to his viewpoint, and the more his friends at the table agree with him, the more your Credible Dissonance meter grows. You aren't sure what to do. If you tend to agree with the political views of the candidate Tom's money is supporting, the more pressure you feel to stay quiet.

"You've read every book and article on the topic for decades, while Tom was building a chain of businesses. But his credibility probably trumps yours, at least in this setting. Now, if you and he were debating in front of the group, things would be different, and you would of course speak up and say more.

"But Credible Dissonance causes a lot of awkward moments.

"There are many other examples. And this brings me to my second concern. Most top politicians will tell you they get a lot of input from successful businessmen, and that much of it is downright wrong. One senator told me he needs the donations of wealthy businessmen to win campaigns, but that nearly all the advice he gets from most business leaders is devoid of an understanding of history and what policies have already been tried.

"There are a few exceptions—business leaders who know their history and policy and really understand what is needed and how to implement it—and the senator listens carefully to such leaders and seeks their counsel on important issues. But again, such business leaders are often the exception.

"That's my second issue. If we get business leaders to engage freedom, but they don't read widely and deeply and understand history, policy, and governance, this freedom project won't be successful."

Both men stood and continued hiking. The trail switchbacked up the mountain, through the trees, and then back past the ski lift.

"So our leaders must be readers," David said.

"Yes. And that's easier said than done. In fact, this idea that the business leaders must actively engage freedom isn't a new one. It's been tried before, but it always breaks down on this point of deep reading. Mortimer Adler and Robert Hutchins, the editors of the *Great Books of the Western World* set, had the same idea as you and published these books for this very purpose.

"But while many business leaders have *The Great Books* or *The Harvard Classics* prominently displayed on their bookshelves, few have read them the way Jefferson, Madison, and most of their generation did. Adler taught numerous seminars and workshops on freedom and leadership for business leaders in cities around the nation, but most of the businessmen who attended were too busy in their jobs to get involved long-term.

"Hutchins was president of the University of Chicago, and he tried to do the same kind of leadership training at the college level. But, again, most of the graduates put their focus on their careers rather than the freedom project.

"Such a project was tried again by Pierre Goodrich, who created a huge endowment to publish important books on freedom and hold seminars about freedom to be attended by leaders from around the nation. The books are some of the most important in history, and because of this fund they are available to all.

"But, sadly, I think they are read mainly by scholars rather than by most of the top business and political leaders. The two freedom seminars I attended by this group were made up of nearly all professors and other academics. If there were successful business leaders in the two groups, I didn't meet any.

"So we've got our work cut out for us. Kami brought me up to speed on your discussions in San Diego, and I agree with your goals. But it isn't going to be easy."

David stopped to get another drink of water, and Wendell leaned against a tree. They were close enough to the ski lift that they could hear the movement of the cable through the trees, but they couldn't see it.

"I wonder why the ski lifts run during the summer," David said.

Wendell laughed, then he responded, "Actually, for some reason they do. I come to Park City several times a year, and these are always running. A lot of people use them to take their mountain bikes to the top and then bike down the trails. Not all ski resorts boast such great views and bike trails, but that's just part of the appeal of this area."

David nodded, but he kept thinking about what Wendell had said earlier. "So, let me get this right," he said, catching his breath in the thin Rocky Mountain air. "You acknowledge three concerns we need to overcome. The first is that we need to attract entrepreneurial-minded leaders, not just those focused on being Credentialists. And the second is that our business leaders need to be deep readers, right?"

"Exactly," Wendell affirmed. "But note that there are many reporters, journalists, entertainers, professors, attorneys, accountants, engineers, and others who are Creators and Builders and should be part of the freedom project, too. And quite a few of them are deep readers. I hope I didn't communicate that reporters for the *Times* or political aides are all Credentialists or Bureaucrats. Many of them are exactly the kind of leaders we'll need."

"Probably 10 percent of them," David said, "given Sturgeon's Law."

Wendell smiled and stood. "Actually, the whole 10 percent thing is the third problem."

20

"Okay, group. You have joined one of the most important teams anywhere. This is going to be some of the hardest work you've ever done."

James paused. "And some of the most rewarding, fun, interesting, and exciting."

More silence from the group.

"But the real point is this. It's going to be successful. We'll keep working until it is. In fact, we've already been at it now for over a century."

The trail narrowed, and David waved to Wendell to go on ahead. As they hiked up the steepest incline yet, David tried to remember everything Kami had told him about Wendell's background.

Wendell Olsen had founded the John Adams Institute for Freedom over two decades ago. The Institute was a think tank focused on using the best wisdom of the past to develop proposals for effective policy changes for current governments. While the Institute's projects dealt with local, state, and national levels, the growth area was consulting governments around the world on how to restructure themselves in order to increase their prosperity and world influence.

The Institute wasn't part of the established network of think tanks that relied mostly on specialists, but rather used the great classics and writings of history as a source of wisdom and then applied it to current affairs. Wendell hired entrepreneurs and set them to influencing the Great Conversation.

While she was an undergraduate student, Kami had read a book written by Wendell and contacted him to request his mentoring. He had met with her frequently while she went through school, and later as she worked for a year as a teacher at a private school and then as a speaker and an account director for a consulting firm.

When he felt she had enough corporate experience, he shook up her world by telling her that she needed to stop thinking like a corporate climber and that she needed to go get sales experience. In four years, she built a network marketing business that made her independently wealthy. Still in her midtwenties, she continued to lead her independent business even as Wendell recommended that she get back into the corporate world.

"You learned a lot in a corporation before," he had told her, "but that was the simplicity on this side of complexity. Now, having become a successful business leader in your own network business, two years of experience back in the corporate world will teach you the simplicity on the other side of complexity."

Kami knew this idea came from a famous quote, but she wasn't sure what he meant. Still, it had felt right, so she got a job at a corporation in San Diego. Less than a year later, the struggling business brought in Indytech, and she met Marcus and David.

By that point, she had come to understand her mentor's cryptic counsel about simplicity and complexity. As a successful business owner herself, she learned so much more than she had ever known about business as she watched the big corporation struggle. She had tried to help with a turnaround, but by the time she got involved the company had already decided to bring in David and his team.

In any case, Wendell had a long expertise in both government principles and entrepreneurship. *So does Kami, for that matter,* David noted.

At the end of the meeting in San Diego, Kami had suggested this longer retreat to take the American turnaround plan to a whole new level. David had offered her the job of putting it all together, just ten minutes after Marcus offered her a role as head of the San Diego corporation they were turning around.

This had all been a difficult decision for Kami, who already had a full-time focus with her growing network marketing business. Ultimately, after a long talk with Wendell, Kami had gone with her passion—and here they all were at a ski resort preparing for tomorrow's retreat.

The fact that it was summer at this ski resort, and that all the snow was gone, wasn't lost on David. The symbolism was they were here to work, not necessarily have fun. Kami had suggested that he and Wendell come a day early and hike the mountain together.

When the trail broadened again, David jogged ahead to catch up with Wendell. "Kami has put together quite a group for this retreat," he said.

"Kami does everything well," Wendell replied. "But yes, it's a good group. I especially like that she kept it small. Most first-time retreat planners bring in too many people, and the quality of the whole thing suffers. Of course, she's done a lot of similar events with her network marketing company."

"You are a real student of human nature, aren't you?" David mused. The men exchanged a glance and smiled.

"I think that's a major part of leadership and in pretty much any setting."

After a few moments, David asked, "So, what's the third issue? You said something about the 10 percent..."

"Yes, but it's not what you think. It's not about whether the 10 percent is accurate or not. Kami told me about your long discussion of the numbers: 10 percent, 3 percent, 14 million, one in a thousand, etc. But this is something else."

"What is it?" David asked.

"In a word, *elitism*. Elitism can shut down our success if we don't approach it wisely."

David looked so quizzically at Wendell that they both broke into laughter.

"Okay," Wendell said, "here's the thing. The truth is, business is very elitist. It is also the opposite of elitist. Business is based on market competition, which means that the buyer gets the best product for the best price. So while the supplier is elitist, a free market naturally creates a democratic result for the consumers.

"Beyond that, consumers like companies that provide the best service for the best price, or in other words, they like a little elitism in the businesses they frequent. Nobody wants to say that they bought the most democratic, mediocre, low-quality pair of shoes or bag of groceries. We all want the best food and other products available. If we hire an accountant, we want her to be the best of the best, not the most equitable.

"Furthermore, nobody really wants to work for a mediocre company, a mediocre boss, or average pay. Business is by nature elitist in that it wants only the best. It is also antielitist in that it wants everyone to participate—the more customers or clients, in most cases, the higher the financial returns.

"But business leaders often have a problem influencing politics because they tend to speak in elitist terms. This drives bureaucratic-minded people crazy, and it is extremely motivating to the Credentialists. This is the one major area in which the Bureaucrats and Credentialists aren't on the same page. When you tell bureaucratic-minded people about Sturgeon's Law and the need for better leadership from the 10 percent, they see you as an elitist, greedy, Wall Street 'rule breaker' or some kind of upstart.

"When you tell Credentialists about Sturgeon's Law and the 10 percent, they immediately see themselves as part of the 10 percent, regardless of whether they actually are, based not on their personal contribution to society but on their view of their own credentials, whatever they are. Then they start trying to figure out how helping freedom can directly impact their current goals—from promotion to a raise to positive PR.

"In contrast," Wendell said as they walked, "Creators want to know how the businesses they've already started can help spread freedom and prosperity, and Builders wonder how they can become part of the 10 percent because they really want to make a positive difference."

The trail was very steep now, and though both men were in good shape they winded quickly. When the trail opened into a large clearing, they both took in a deep breath at the panoramic view of the valley below. They could literally see for miles.

"Have you been to Park City before?" David asked.

"Yes, a few times." Wendell was breathing hard. "Not enough, though. Look at that view…"

Both men sat down on large boulders and enjoyed the light mountain breeze. "The American turnaround project isn't elitist," Wendell said between breaths. "The whole point is that elites in Washington and Wall Street run nearly everything, and as a result our freedoms are decreasing. The divide between the rich and the rest just keeps growing, and in a truly free society that doesn't happen."

"Under true free enterprise," David added, "everyone has opportunity."

21

Josh was excited. "They're going deeper, Mr. President."

"Yes. But will they be able to communicate this much depth to the people of their time?" James sighed. "And, on the other hand, will they ever get deep enough to really understand what is needed? They're so far behind our generation."

James saw Josh looking at him, and he smiled. "I know, Josh. That's too arrogant. In many ways, they're ahead. But on the issue of depth, they really are behind. And it may be their Achilles' heel."

The problem is that business leaders are accustomed to using the language of elitism," Wendell continued, "so the people in the nation end up thinking that the 10 percent are trying to take away democracy and freedom. The truth is exactly the opposite. The 10 percent are really just caring, regular citizens who happen to have business leadership skills. But as long as they talk like elitists, many of the people won't trust them.

"The irony is that the real elites, the ones who *want* to increase the divide between themselves and the masses, have learned through history how to speak the language of democracy. They are actually more like aristocrats than elitists, but they are educated on how to sway things so they end up winning. In fact, they are educated in history, the great classics, and great literature, so they know exactly what to say to get the support of the masses."

"Literature?" David asked with a hint of concern in his voice.

Wendell laughed. They were both catching their breath now. "When most business leaders think of literature, they think of Jane Austen, *Jane Eyre*, and all that. But what do you think literature actually is? It's the history of how to effectively spin things. It teaches how the greatest storytellers of history got the masses to agree with them.

"For example, Jane Austen convinced the masses that they were just as important as the aristocrats, and that wit, character, and doing the right thing even in hard situations is what makes people great—not one's birth, social class, money, or education. She was one of the original proponents of performance over bureaucracy, credentialism, and elitism. Literature is powerful, and it is the language of the masses.

"Of course, the mass language of Austen's day isn't the language of the masses today. But popular authors in each time period are popular precisely because they catch the imagination of the people. It's helpful for thinking leaders to look at popular literature as an important and effective way of understanding the general populace.

"In our specialized modern world, most leaders aren't trained to think of it this way, but it's an interesting way to look at things. Steve Jobs was reported in the *New York Times* as being a lifetime student of the writings of William Blake, and Visa founder Dee Hock put writers like John Steinbeck and Wallace Stegner to similar use. Eventually, Hock came to consider Omar Khayyam's *Rubaiyat* the most helpful work of literature.

"Nike founder Phil Knight also built a large personal library of literature and poetry. In his book *First Things First*, Stephen Covey called this consistent approach of learning leadership from the great books by its own title: wisdom literature.

"Of course, there's more to the classics than the language of the masses, but this is one of their important contributions.

"Many business leaders today are well-trained in their profession, and they know how to speak the language of the professions. If they get involved in politics, they have to learn to speak the languages of history and governing as well. But few of them know how to effectively speak the language of the masses.

"In contrast, the true elitists teach their kids the language of history and policy through the classics, but they also make sure they know the language of the masses by reading lots of great literature and other books and materials."

"That's very interesting," David said. "So my wife is way ahead of me on this?"

Wendell grinned. "Actually, the most important point isn't that leaders can understand the heart of the masses by reading Austen, but that the masses can understand the heart of leadership by doing so."

After a long pause, David asked, "So, the citizen-leaders speak like elitists while they try to spread freedom... and the aristocratic-elites speak like supporters of democracy while they're swaying the masses to give up freedom?"

"Exactly. That's the history of the world. It's also the history of the United States. As Tocqueville said in *Democracy in America*, history is the battle between supporters of aristocracy and promoters of democracy. More specifically, this is exactly what happened to American freedom in 1913."

"That's right," David said. "Many elites hated the Senate, because senators were elected by each state legislature and kept the elites from passing all their programs to bring more of the masses' money to Washington and Wall Street. So the elites told the people to make the Senate more democratic by passing the Seventeenth Amendment.

"Once it passed, senators were elected directly by the people, and the elites were able to take away most of the powers of the states and move them to the federal government. That never could have happened if the senators were still appointed by state legislatures."

Wendell nodded. "Yes, and then the elites got Congress to pass laws that made it harder for people without a lot of capital to make more money and made it easier for those with money to increase wealth. Thus we have the increasing division between the rich and the rest ever since."

"And they sold the whole thing by saying that it would make America more democratic. That's so interesting." David shook his head.

Wendell looked out at the valley, then turned to David. "Now, here's my main point. The business leaders and others who participate in the American turnaround project have to use language that works with the masses. They can't actually look for the 10 percent. They have to believe that everyone is capable of being in the 10 percent and invite everyone to participate."

"The truth is that everyone *is* capable of being a leader in the 10 percent," David said, "but under Sturgeon's Law only about 10 percent will actually rise to the occasion."

"Good. We target everyone and know that around 10 percent will take action. But we have to try to attract everyone, as I said, because that's the only way we'll get the best 10 percent. That's entirely antielitist, and we need to truly believe it and stick with it."

"Absolutely," David said firmly. "Because it's true."

Wendell paused, then added, "Actually, our national problem with elitism is really an issue of meritocracy. Jefferson spoke of a natural aristocracy, and many modern Americans have taken his words as a support of meritocracy. But they define meritocracy mostly by credentials rather than performance, as we were discussing earlier.

"In other words, they think that the natural aristocracy is made up of those who have the best résumés, not those who give the greatest service."

David responded, "I just read about this recently: every member of the Supreme Court graduated from an Ivy League school, and nearly all presidential candidates for the past decades did, too. This could be because these schools train the best leaders...but it could also be simply that in our credential-oriented society, we elect based on credentials rather than actual performance."

"Here's another way to look at." Wendell took in a long, deep breath of cool air. "Pew Research Center pointed out that the United States has almost the lowest economic mobility—a person's ability to move from poor to middle class or from middle class to wealthy—of all industrialized nations in the world. Canada is 2.5 times more mobile than the U.S., and Germany is 1.5 times more mobile. Denmark is 3 times more mobile. Only England, the other meritocratic nation, has lower mobility than America."

"Fascinating," David said. "We call ourselves the nation of freedom, but our freedoms are decreasing right in front of our eyes."

"Have you read *Twilight of the Elites* by Christopher Hayes?" Wendell asked.

David shook his head.

"Well, that is where I read these statistics about America's falling levels of economic opportunity. I didn't agree with everything in the book, but it has a lot of valuable information. For example, Hayes talks about the Iron Law of Meritocracy, which is that meritocracy always creates a system of massive inequality because 'merit' is narrowly defined and controlled from the top by experts who work for the elites.

"In fact, Hayes says that our meritocracy isn't very meritocratic at all. Again, it sees credentials as merit, not effective service and performance that truly benefits society. In such a meritocracy, performance isn't valued, and only Credentialists and Bureaucrats thrive. Innovation wanes, and freedom and prosperity decrease.

"The government attacks the 1 percent and uses this as an excuse to take more money from the entrepreneurial sector, while the superwealthy shelter their money in trusts and foundations as well as offshore. In fact, the divide between the masses and the 1 percent hasn't grown as much as the divide between the 1 percent and the .01 percent!

"Even more interesting, the division between the wealth of the .01 percent and the .001 percent is even bigger, and growing. But the fact that the wealthy are making more money isn't the problem; it's the reality that the regular people have less opportunity for success with each passing year."

David took a sandwich out of his small pack. Before he took a bite, he looked Wendell in the eyes and said, "One: entrepreneurial thinkers from all backgrounds. Two: readers of history, the great books, and the classics of literature. Three: speaking the language of the masses."

The two men ate in silence as they pondered. The wind in the quaking aspens filled the high valley with constant sound, similar to running water. After a while, the sun broke over the peaks, and the men took off their outer layers of hiking clothes.

22

"Sir, their whole business leadership genre is really quite profound. Their business literature is full of wisdom that rivals the level of some of our greatest classics."

"True, James. But that's not my concern. It's not what they read. It's more about if they read. But it goes even deeper than that. It's mostly about how they read."

"You're right sir. They tend to read like beginning math students, looking for the right answer, not some nugget of wisdom that might apply to a long list of current questions one is pondering."

"That's my concern, James. We were taught to read like poets, or prophets, seeking inspiration. They were trained to read like accountants—rote, flat."

The tall man looked at James with piercing eyes. "Can you help their reading come alive?"

Do you want to hike all the way to the summit?" David asked.

"Of course," Wendell said enthusiastically, "but maybe that's not the best use of our time. We could ride the ski lift down. I can see the top of it down below. Above us there are no more ski runs, just mountains. Or we can sit here and talk more."

"I don't know about talking anymore." David was uncharacteristically tired. "All these conversations seem to go the same way. We bring up the great need for a new American paradigm shift, everyone agrees and wants to join the project, and then there are long discussions on all the problems and issues we'll face. In truth, it's a little frustrating."

"Imagine doing it for more than twenty years and still facing the same concerns," Wendell said with a big smile.

David realized his gaffe—that Wendell had been working in this field his whole adult life. "Sorry." He grinned. "Every beginner faces some negative thoughts."

"You're no beginner," Wendell said. "You're a pro. You're just applying your wisdom to a new challenge, and admittedly world freedom is not a small goal."

Instead of laughing at the irony of this understatement, David went straight to the point. "Okay, what other key challenges and problems are we facing?"

"Probably a lot, but your team has already cleared one of the most difficult hurdles. You pinpointed the problem, the fact that the Constitution only fully works if a large number of regular citizens stay actively in tune with, and involved in, daily governance. The separation of powers and the system of checks and balances all require this essential and extra, unwritten branch of government— a bunch of highly involved citizen-leaders.

"That's huge progress. It's a significant addition to the Great Conversation, even if we accomplish nothing else.

"It's basically a fourth branch of government, and I don't mean the press, though at its very best that is exactly what journalism accomplishes. But for whatever reason, only a small part of the media is still fulfilling this role, and with so many dissonant media voices, it seems to me that the people have lost their trust in the press anyway.

"Some of the media, the best of them, are deeply supportive of real freedom—in their own way, of course. But we need leaders from all sectors of society to take leadership roles, and we especially need it from the entrepreneurial-minded leaders.

"That's a huge contribution, and you should be proud of what you've already done. That said, we can do more. This retreat will bear fruit."

"So will our time together today," David said. "Thanks for that. But I disagree with one thing you said. A committed group of the people closely watching the government isn't a fourth branch of government—it's actually the *first* branch."

Wendell considered this a bit, then nodded. "Y'know, you're absolutely right."

"Now, what else do you want to talk about?" David asked.

"The big question is how to attract the entrepreneurial-thinking business leaders and other leaders from our society. We can't just put an ad on the nightly news. Or can we? That's our question. How do we reach them? Like your team already realized, these business leaders already care. But how do we get them actively involved and truly engaged? How do we get them to read the court cases, laws, executive orders, treaties, not to mention the great classics and history?

"They're all too busy for all that, or at least that's what they think. That's our problem. How do we get them to buy in to become deeply involved citizens?"

"I've been trying to figure this out ever since San Diego," David said. "So far nothing has clicked. I mean, how did the Founders get so many regular citizens involved?"

"That's the easiest question we've asked in this whole project," Wendell replied.

Surprised, David repeated, "So how did they do it?"

"They taught their children to be involved citizens almost from birth," Wendell said. "And once they learned to do it through childhood and youth, they naturally kept doing it as adults. It was a natural habit for nearly everyone."

Wendell reached for his iPhone and checked to see if he had service this high up the mountain. Then he pulled up a quote from his bookmark. "This came from Samuel Williams, a teacher in Vermont, who wrote it in 1794, just a few years after Washington became the first president of the U.S."

He handed his phone to David and said, "Read this."

David read from the screen:

All the children are trained up to this kind of knowledge: they are accustomed from their earliest years to read the Holy Scriptures, the periodical publications, newspapers, and political pamphlets; to form some general acquaintance with the laws of their country, the proceedings of the courts of justice, of the general assembly of the state, and of the Congress, etc.

Such a kind of education is common and universal in every part of the state: and nothing would be more dishonorable to the parents, or to the children, than to be without it.

After the first time through, David slowed his reading and read it again. When he looked up, Wendell said, "That's all we have to do. Totally restructure our educational system and how we parent and raise up real citizen-leaders. We'll alter the whole nation in one generation."

They both smiled. "If only..." David let his words drift into the wind.

"Since that isn't a realistic option, we have to find something else," Wendell said. "Of course, we can do this in our own families. Kayla and I have done it with all our kids, and a lot of parents do it. But a lot more is needed to turn around the nation, of course. The best book on this subject is *A Thomas Jefferson Education*. In my opinion, it should be required reading in school."

David nodded. "So where do we go from here?"

"Well, when I get frustrated with how much needs to change,

my wife often reminds me that we shouldn't forget the nation's Founders. They had to totally overcome their culture by taking on centuries of the British caste system, a near-religious belief in the divine right of kings, and the universally accepted but false idea that men are not created equal. It was hard work, but they did it. Our task is no more difficult than theirs."

David pondered this thought, then nodded. "I hadn't considered it in that way."

"Besides," Wendell continued, "we've made significant progress. We know *who*, and we know *what*." Wendell turned off his phone and put it back into his pack.

David stood and threw a rock far down the clearing. "Business leaders, parents, and other regular citizens are the *who*, and the *what* is getting them to read the great classics and history, and get actively involved in studying what the government is doing each day and using their influence to sway it in the right direction.

"That's big... really big."

David smiled and turned to Wendell. All feelings of frustration were gone. " 'There is no magic in small dreams...,' " he quoted. "This is the most overwhelming, most ridiculously hard, most incredibly exciting thing I've ever done! I mean, if we succeed, the whole world will change..."

Wendell rose, and the two men looked out at the panorama.

"Y'know, it's a lot like than golf," Wendell said drily. "Impossibly hard, amazingly fun. The challenge of a lifetime. Let's do it."

They both laughed heartily at the silly comparison. But the point was made.

The two regarded the panoramic view once more, then turned and headed up the trail toward the summit.

23

*"This is the perfect place for their retreat," Josh said, "so I worked
hard to make sure they had every opportunity to book it. The way
the sky and mountain and trees reflect off the big pool—I think it's
an incredibly inspiring setting, Mr. President."*

"Excellent," James said.

The way to get entrepreneurial-minded leaders to become
actively engaged citizens is to make it worth their time," Wendell
said as they climbed. "To accomplish that we have to know what
they want."

"I've been thinking a lot about that," David said.

"What have you come up with?"

"Well, you know about real business motivation coming at the
intersection of passion, potential, and profit, right?"

Wendell nodded.

"Well, as various philosophers ultimately figured out, all people want success. Some great thinkers have felt that people merely
want happiness, but their arguments don't persuade. It seems that as
soon as a person attains what he considers to be happiness, he very
quickly begins looking for something new to seek after.

"What does he seek? Some kind of success. It might be financial, romantic, fun, pleasure, or some other kind of success, but it's
always success we humans want. We define it differently, but we all

want it. What I haven't yet figured out is exactly how knowing that most people want success helps us. Any ideas?"

"I'm not sure." Wendell pondered this as he walked. "I read somewhere that there are five major paths to success. Maybe we can learn something from this. The first path, if I'm remembering it correctly, is money or financial success. Then there is knowledge success, and the third is power success. Each of these is pretty self-explanatory.

"But the interesting thing is that each of these paths creates a different set of strengths, skills, weaknesses, and views of the world. For example, there are a lot of similarities among people who've achieved knowledge success, but they are quite different than those who obtained money success. And those who've gained power success have significant differences from the other two.

"The point is this: most people who work hard and obtain knowledge success eventually find themselves also wanting money success. So many successful academics, journalists, and people from other top knowledge fields spend years obtaining great knowledge and then feel that they should be more highly compensated for what they know.

"In contrast, those whose hard work over time leads to financial success frequently find that they desire more power. They have the money, and they've always believed that money is power. But actually, political power is political power—meaning that political office and direct political influence have more sway than money in many cases, especially when a major political action is needed or a big choice has to be made in Washington or other seats of government.

"At the top level of things, political power isn't easily purchased no matter how much money you have, as people like Ross Perot, Steve Jobs, George Soros, Donald Trump, and others have all discovered.

"Finally, those with power success find that they never quite have enough knowledge. They want to know and understand more, and thus people with real political power success often turn to seeking greater knowledge."

David was soaking in these ideas. He didn't agree with everything, but he was enjoying the intellectual bent of the conversation. He had spent so many years as the leader in every setting, it was actually pleasurable to sit back and enjoy the discussion.

Both men kept climbing.

"But there are two other major paths to success," Wendell continued. "One is position power, which comes from one's official title or status. Many with Credentialist or Bureaucratic mentalities follow this path. The sad thing is that when those seeking position power achieve a coveted position, their immediate goal is usually to seek a higher position.

"This is a consuming and unrewarding path, because every position is immediately seen as just a stepping stone to something better, something which can never truly arrive."

"That reminds me of 'The Inner Ring,' a lecture by C. S. Lewis," David said.

"Oh, that happens to be one of my all-time favorites," Wendell responded, "and it leads directly to the last major path of success, which is wisdom. When people find wisdom, they naturally want more wisdom. And increased wisdom allows them more influence on things.

"Also, people who seem to be on the money path may actually be on the position path or the wisdom path. Likewise, when it seems like someone is pursuing the knowledge or the power path, he or she may really be seeking position or wisdom.

"So, to summarize, the business leaders and the other top leaders who we want to become super-involved citizens will likely come from all these paths, but we've got to help them move toward the path of wisdom. This doesn't mean they have to give up their other goals, because more wisdom will actually help them succeed more on the paths of knowledge, money, or power."

Wendell stopped talking and kept walking toward the summit. The sun was high now, and both men had stripped down to T-shirts and shorts. Their sweat dripped on their hiking boots as they continued their trek.

Hours later, shortly before noon, they walked out of the forest onto the bare land above the timberline. They could see the trail winding up to the peak, and they realized another hour of hiking was still ahead. After a few minutes they reached a steep, rocky part of the trail. When they reached the top of the rocks, they sat down and rested a bit before going on.

The wind was cooler this high up the mountain, and the views were even more spectacular than those they had enjoyed earlier. After they both caught their breath, they sat enjoying the silence.

"Look at that huge tree," marveled Wendell.

David had noticed it when they first reached the timberline, a large tree that stood alone on a grassy slope far above the rest of the forest.

"It stands there like a leader to all the others," said David. "It's most impressive."

"Imagine how strong it has to be to withstand so much snow every winter..."

"Leadership can be daunting—and lonely," David agreed. "But it is so rewarding, and the challenges make you strong."

They were silent again for a time, and neither moved to hike again.

Finally, Wendell broke the silence. "Y'know, I read your book a couple of years ago. I thought it was one of the best in the leadership genre. And I've read all your books since."

"Thank you," David replied. "I must say I've loved reading your books, too. I really enjoyed sharing your book on the American Founders with the leaders in my company. When Kami said she wanted to invite you to the retreat, I was excited about meeting you."

"I called some of my most successful business friends," Wendell said, "and they all either knew you or knew of you. Daniel Carrigan, the billionaire investor who is almost as big as Warren Buffett, said you were the world's leading turnaround expert. When I asked about you, he assured me you can turn any company to success because you are a genius at identifying exactly what is wrong in a very short time and then helping the company do precisely what is needed."

David was pleased, but he felt humbled by the praise. "It's all about the Five Laws of Decline," he said. "They really are the key. Once someone really understands the laws and knows exactly what to look for, it's like clockwork. You just identify where the company is weak using the Five Laws, and you get to work figuring out how to overcome the problems."

"I know where you discovered the laws," Wendell said, "because you named them after their creators, like Theodore Sturgeon and Frédéric Bastiat. But where did you get the idea to put them together in a system?"

"Actually, once I got really interested in reading the greatest books, the laws just naturally fell into place. When Monte and I were just getting started with Indytech, we began consulting them to overcome difficult challenges in the companies we helped, and they worked so well that over time we learned to focus on them right at the beginning of any turnaround.

"Then, one day, while Monte and I were discussing how incredibly effective they are, we ended up relating them to the idea of fallen man. It's interesting how flawed, fallen man tends to make mistakes in exactly the ways described by the Five Laws of Decline."

"Evil, too," nodded Wendell. "The laws explain how people like Hitler or Mao could get an entire nation to follow them."

"Exactly," continued David. "When humans create a new organization, and it grows to become something good and important, it naturally faces human weakness, whether by design from those seeking evil or, even more often, just the mistakes of those involved. Either way, the Five Laws account for nearly all ways in which we human beings seem to struggle."

"So it ties in biblically," Wendell said, "even though that isn't where you originally found it."

"Yes. And it's also found in the Talmud, the Vedas, and the teachings of other world religions."

"The Qur'an too," Wendell noted, "and in the writings of Confucius. Also in Plato and Aristotle. The Five Laws show up almost universally in the great wisdom literature. And you've adapted it to the world of business. When I asked several other friends about you, including a couple of Forbes 400 leaders, they all said something similar . . . about you being able to see precisely what is needed to fix any organization.

"In fact, my friend Carey Allen at Ohio State sent me a file of articles she had collected about you and how your techniques have succeeded—from *Sloan Management Review*, the Young Presidents' Organization, and *Fortune* magazine. Also a speech you gave that was printed in *Vital Speeches of the Day*, and several other clippings. You really are *the* leading expert on turnarounds."

"The Five Laws are that profound," David said.

Both men stretched their calves by leaning against the steep rocks, then they headed up the trail. It was time to keep pushing onward.

24

"I was surprised when you quoted Tocqueville to them, Mr. President," Josh said, as they watched the two men climb the steep slope. "You usually don't quote sources that came after the founding..."

James chuckled. "That needs to change. Wisdom is wisdom, whatever its source."

They finally reached the summit in the early afternoon. They sat in silence for almost an hour, enjoying the view and the clean air. Their only companions were occasional birds and the white jet streams of airplanes high above.

"Have you found it difficult to apply your expertise with the Five Laws to the United States?" Wendell asked. "I mean, a nation is much bigger than a company."

"Well, yes and no. It was very simple to pinpoint the problems. The Five Laws are extremely powerful, and they apply so effectively to any human organization, big or small. If there is decline, the Five Laws are at work. That's what makes them laws, and I've learned that they really are this exact.

"The second step of outlining what solutions will work was also simple. Not easy, but simple. I just asked if we are in decline, why we are in decline, where the Five Laws are hurting us, and how we could fix government or society so the Five Laws aren't perpetuating damage."

"That's how you realized that the 10 percent weren't doing their part, right?"

"Yes. That's the biggest problem. But there is another major concern as well. As long as you allow people to vote in their own self-benefits, the government will vote itself bankrupt and eventually out of existence. There are no exceptions in history, unless the 10 percent can figure this out and change it before it's too late."

Wendell smiled. "Tocqueville wrote the same thing. And others, too. In fact, a famous quote sometimes attributed to Alexander Tytler is that 'a Democracy . . . can only exist until the voters discover they can vote themselves largesse from the public treasury. From that moment on, the majority always votes for the candidate promising them the most benefits.'

"It gets back to your comments about the Five Laws being a business way of explaining the idea of fallen man. Or, in secular terms, flawed man."

"Madison said the same thing—that if men were angels we'd have no need for government."

"Right," said Wendell. "In fact, in *Federalist Paper* 51 where he says that, he also teaches that government is just a reflection of human nature. The same is true of all human organizations, which makes your system of using the Five Laws so effective."

David agreed. "That thought by Madison about if men were angels is quoted a lot, but what most people don't remember is that the very next point he makes in *Federalist* 51 is that the government must be overseen by the people. And if the people ever stop overseeing the government, freedom will be lost."

"The exact word Madison uses is *dependence*," Wendell said, warming to the conversation, "meaning that a people who closely watch their government is the primary control on government abuse."

"The Framers got so much right," said David. "Our freedoms today would not exist without their sacrifice, study, and inspiration. But they left a few weaknesses, and given human nature the

Five Laws always find weaknesses and use them to cause decline. If only I could have talked to James Madison about the Five Laws of Decline..."

Wendell chuckled at the thought. "Maybe that should be our plan, to build a time-travel machine and go have a talk with him just before the Constitutional Convention."

"Perfect." David laughed with him. "Just a few tweaks, and the Five Laws couldn't have gotten any traction."

"What tweaks?" Wendell's face turned serious.

"Actually, I've put a lot of thought into this, and I've written up a proposal to present to the group. Like I said, the Framers got so much right, but they allowed loopholes that eventually led to significant losses of freedom. I know it's immodest for me to say this... but I think a few key changes to their system would fix the nation."

"How did you come up with the idea of applying the Five Laws to our nation?"

"Actually, that was a major turning point in my life. I was reading the works of Bertrand de Jouvenel, published by Liberty Fund, and I was struck by his ideas on how freedom really works. Around the same time, I read books by several thinkers in the Austrian Economics school of thought, including Murray Rothbard and Hans-Hermann Hoppe, and I kept noticing the Five Laws in all these commentaries on government and economics.

"One day, while I was reading from de Jouvenel, I found myself writing notes on how to apply the Five Laws to political leadership. When I realized what I was doing, it was truly a major paradigm shift. It dawned on me that the problems of our nation are based on the Five Laws just as much as the businesses I've helped fix over the years.

"I was so excited that I immediately pulled out my notebook and started writing out questions, answers, and solutions for modern concerns. Almost everyone in our world today realizes that something is broken in our society, and that voting in elections seldom brings the kinds of changes we really need. When I discovered that the Five Laws were totally applicable to our governmental, economic, and national challenges, it was natural to start outlining effective solutions. I asked myself where the Five Laws were hurting our nation, and how we could fix government so this would stop."

"And, as a top expert on the Five Laws and successful turn-arounds," Wendell added, "you realized how unique and potentially influential the Five Laws might be for our country."

"Yes. I thought of all the organizations we had turned around, and it was clear that our national problems were explained by the Five Laws. But hardly anyone knows the laws well enough to use them at this scale. That's when I got really excited and started taking copious notes on this freedom project."

"This is exciting," Wendell enthused.

"The hard part is getting today's citizens excited about it."

"Why do you think that's such a problem?"

"I'm not sure," David said, "but a big part of it is overspecialization. We have stopped being a nation of closely involved citizen-leaders who are broadly educated on government and leadership, and yet we've become a nation of experts.

"Now, don't get me wrong. Expertise has an important place in any advanced economy, but we've taken it so far that even many of the best experts are highly dependent on other experts for anything outside their specialty. The result is that people defer to the experts on almost anything, so getting the 10 percent to lead in government is a major challenge, because business leaders will wonder why the political experts don't just do it."

Wendell responded, "That's why we haven't yet applied the Five Laws to government and the economy, because the laws come from different specialties. So few experts in any field have the benefit of seeing how all five work together in our nation's problems."

"That's right. Just try to suggest a solution that draws from multiple specialties. The experts fight it because they have no idea what's going on. It is a major cause of business dysfunction, and it makes it much more difficult to lead an effective organizational turnaround. The top experts from different departments have a very hard time looking past their own fiefdoms of specialty and cooperating to turn things around—even when they all realize how bad things are."

"On a national level, it's even more of a problem," Wendell said with a nod, "because the specialists from many fields mistrust each other and also tend to tear down any who try to intermingle the specialties. The ancient philosophers called such out-of-the-box thinking wisdom, but today's experts just see people who don't speak the right specialized jargon."

"It's the same Credible Dissonance you talked about this morning," David said.

Wendell stood and lifted his small pack. "But the difference occurs when somebody has enough expertise and depth in the multiple specialties—in this case the Five Laws—to lead all specialties. And that's why this project just might succeed."

The wind picked up, and David stood. Both men started down the trail. They walked slowly, each lost in his thoughts. When they reached the top of the ski lift, they grabbed a chair and rode the rest of the way down.

"Wisdom really is the whole point," David said, referring back to one of the topics from that morning. "And the habits and skills of wisdom are not always the same as those learned from the other kinds of success. It's an additional ability, but a vital one.

"It's a tall order for most people, at least in our modern world where we don't teach these values or skills to our children." David closed his eyes and enjoyed the feeling of the breeze on his face as he rode the lift toward the valley.

Wendell drank the last water from his bottle, and then he smiled at David. "This was a good day," he said.

"Definitely."

PART III

25

"The second team is in place, Mr. President. What year do you want them to start with?"

"I don't want to dictate to them. Have them discuss and decide which year is the right place to start."

"It would help if I could tell them what they're looking for, Mr. President."

"Ask them to consider what they think they should look for, Josh."

When Josh left the room, James put down the book he was reading. "'Leadership by Wandering Around.' What a great idea," he said aloud.

Thank you, Kami," David told the group. "That was an excellent summary of where we're at. Our nation is experiencing all the problems that come with all Five Laws of Decline, we need more truly involved citizen-leaders, and we've got to attract them to their leadership roles. Moreover, we think a lot of them will come from business leadership, and that a top attractor for such leaders will be some combination of money, knowledge, power, and wisdom.

"Beyond that, we're not sure what to do next. How do we get about one in a thousand Americans, at least two hundred thousand people, to voluntarily step up and become the kind of leaders who can help the rest of the people turn our society in the right direction?

How do we get them to closely read about and follow our government and influence its direction on a daily, weekly, and ongoing basis?"

"I like the way you said it that time," Monte interrupted. "Instead of using the word *turnaround*, which sort of communicates that we should go backward, I like the idea of turning toward the right direction. Sure, we want to adopt the best things from the past, but we don't want to go backward. Not at all. We want to go forward, but turned toward a better trajectory."

"That's a good clarification," David said. "So, it's time to discuss. Let's have an informal discussion without any rules to bog us down. The time is now yours to go wherever we need in order to help turn America toward a better path to freedom and prosperity."

David sat down, and Marcus immediately spoke up. "At first, I thought this whole freedom thing was a bit cheesy. I mean, we elect leaders to handle our freedoms, right? But after our last meeting in San Diego, I can't stop thinking about all this. I mean, even if our freedoms decrease, I know I can still make a place for myself and be successful.

"But I don't want to make it harder for my kids someday, if I have kids. I mean, I want to have a family at some point, and I don't want my kids to grow up in a world with less freedom. Or to have my kids raise their children in such a place."

Marcus paused. "Somehow this freedom thing has really got me intrigued. For those of you who don't know me, I really like luxury watches..." He had to wait for those who *did* know him to stop laughing. Then he continued, "Well, after thinking about all this following our meeting in San Diego, I decided to do something to help freedom. So I sold one of my watches on eBay. It was an A. Lange and Söhne platinum Moonphase, and it sold for $39,988." He paused to be sure that everyone was noticing his attention to detail. "Then I searched for places online to donate the money to help freedom."

Marcus looked around the room. "To tell the truth, I'm a little embarrassed about this, but I'm not sure why. I guess I'm breaking with my Ayn Rand view of life. Also, I couldn't decide what to do with this money that would really make a difference. So, if any of you have suggestions for me, I'm still looking." Marcus sat down.

Everyone sat in silence for a few moments.

"David," Michelle finally said, "I think it was extremely helpful in San Diego when you applied proven business principles to the freedom issue."

"I agree," Kami said enthusiastically. "That's what makes this group so unique. We're not looking to promote a certain political candidate, but to help rebuild a truly vital branch of government—the active citizens who keep a close eye on government and help everyone else keep it in its proper place."

"What will effectively attract the needed leaders to start being a different kind of citizen?" David asked.

Luke raised his hand, and David called on him to speak.

Kami had introduced everyone in the group earlier. Luke DiCastro was a self-made oil billionaire and Wall Street investor. He had a love for small institutions and businesses with great ideas but limited capital, and he kept a purposely low profile so he could walk into such organizations, seek a low-paying job or volunteer role, and work for a few months to get the feel of the people, plans, and leaders.

If he liked what he saw, he offered the organization professional business planning, capital and financial management, and whatever else it needed to succeed. His unique method of investing had made him extremely successful.

Spencer Boardman had served four terms as a Democratic senator from the state of Missouri, and he had just retired from a long career as an attorney. He also spoke fluent Mandarin and had worked on numerous international trade negations representing Chinese firms. When Kami suggested his involvement, David had agreed that his experience in the legal and political trenches would be invaluable to the group.

"Are we planning to actually do something, or is this more of an academic discussion?" Luke asked. "I'm game for either, but if we really want to somehow engage a million new serious, unelected leaders, I'm totally in."

"That's precisely what we want," David affirmed. "The question is, how do we do it?"

"Yes, Senator?" Kami said when Spencer raised his hand.

"Please, call me Spence."

"Excellent, Spence."

"About your question... Actually, I think the real question is *how can it be done*, not how *we* can do it, right?" Spence asked. "Is this about us doing it, or about the fact that it needs to be done?"

"It doesn't have to be us, Spence," Kami said, as David, Monte, and others nodded.

"I think it would be great if someone else did it. That's my vote," Marcus glibly announced. "I'll use my eBay money toward another watch. I've had my eye on a Girard-Perregaux watch, a platinum Perpetual Calendar Ferrari F50 Limited Edition for $95,000..."

"That sounds like it has a lot of horsepower," Monte joked.

"I know one thing that will work," Wendell said, all business. "We can do nothing, let freedom and prosperity continue to deteriorate, and just watch the nation decline. Eventually things will get bad enough that citizens and business leaders will have to turn their attention to government and do something."

Marcus stopped thinking about watches and shook his head angrily. "But by that point it might be too late to turn things in the right direction. We can't do *nothing*, not when we know the problems and that we need to fix them. Plus, I doubt anyone is going to be able to fix things unless they understand the Five Laws."

Wendell nodded. "I only said that to show how important it is to take action. Of course we shouldn't wait for things to get worse.

The truth is the current levels of government overreach are already seriously dampening the entrepreneurial spirit that made America great. And things are getting worse over time regardless of elections."

"Most innovation comes from small business, not big corporations," Monte added, "and the majority of small entrepreneurs can't afford to keep fighting this uphill battle against increasing regulation and government interference. Time is short, and we need to act."

"The question is, what to do?" Spence said. "What will really work? How can we get hundreds of thousands of business leaders, parents, and other regular citizens to step up and become fully engaged leaders?"

The conversation continued, but it didn't seem to get anywhere. David finally called for a break.

26

"They're struggling, Josh. We need to help them."

"Yes, Mr. President. I'll call an emergency meeting and get right on it."

Luke started right in as soon as everyone was seated. "My guiding principle of business is something I read once. I think—it was Peter Drucker who said it: starve the problems and feed the opportunities."

His energy was electric, and everyone sat up straighter in their chairs.

"In Kami's introduction, David's overview of the project, and Wendell's comments to me during the break, the focus is on all the challenges we'll have to overcome to succeed in an American turnaround."

He looked around the room, and the pause caused everyone to look at him more closely.

"I think we should start focusing on the opportunities. Who cares if there will be challenges? Of course there will be. There are obstacles to any worthy endeavor. That's a given. But leadership is about opportunities. Let's put all of our energies, creativity, and mind power into the possibilities."

David leaned forward in his chair. "That's so right. It's all about vision. What kind of America do we want to move toward?

What's the goal?" David had guided a lot of discussions like this, and he knew it was vital to strike quickly when such energy spread through the group. "What if we backed up and looked at this in a whole new way?" he asked.

The synergy in the room was palpable.

"Can I make a suggestion?" Kami asked. "What if we visualize ourselves during the time of the Founding Fathers, just for the sake of clarifying what we really want for America—and then consider how to change the Constitution in a way that the 10 percent would never stop doing their job? Sort of a simulation, but one that would directly address our purpose."

"I love it!" Monte exclaimed. "A dress rehearsal of sorts!" Everyone nodded.

Kami walked to the whiteboard. "Let's brainstorm. What could the Founders have added to or taken from the Constitution that would change history in such a way that today, over two centuries later, the 10 percent would be actively and voluntarily engaged in daily governance of our nation?"

"That also kept the business leaders highly involved," Marcus added.

"And mothers and fathers," Michelle added.

"Wait," Wendell said in surprise. "This is amazing, but I think I'm having a breakthrough." His enthusiasm was contagious and everyone leaned forward in anticipation while he quickly collected his thoughts.

"Okay, this is big. The Founders didn't write about it because it was just the world they lived in, so they didn't see the need to make it part of the Constitution. And since it was local, it wasn't really relevant in a federal Constitution anyway. But the Constitution was based on the local system of government, and in fact the Constitution could not have been written as it was or implemented without the local system of that time.

"Most modern Americans don't think a lot about the

Constitution. They just take their freedoms for granted because they have always had them..."

"Like a fish in water," David said. "The fish is the last one to notice the water. He just swims around and enjoys the benefits of water, and only realizes how important it is when he is taken out of it. When that happens, he'll give anything to have the water again."

"That reminds me of Plato's parable of the cave," Kami said.

"Or *Pride and Prejudice*." Amy was getting excited. "We don't know what we don't know, until something forces us out of our normal comfort zone and we realize how blind we've been to something very important. Then we realize that our pride, prejudice, and lack of sensibility have kept us from seeing something that really matters."

"Exactly," Wendell continued. "Well, the Founders didn't give much thought to the local system of government. They just took it for granted, like David's fish. But, like I said, the whole constitutional system was based on it. So today, when we've entirely lost the local system they enjoyed, we see the Constitution struggling to maintain our freedoms and we wonder what went wrong."

"We can blame it on changes to the Constitution, like those in 1913 or the others we discussed in San Diego," Kami said, "but David was correct that ultimately the fault lies in the fact that the 10 percent stopped doing their job of watching and consistently influencing the government. When the regular, everyday people stop being a check on government, it surges out of control. There is no exception to this, not in all the history of free governments."

"Tell us more, Wendell." David was clearly intrigued.

"Well, when the first colonists organized small towns and communities in the Americas, they set up local governments to oversee themselves. Tocqueville wrote about it in *Democracy in America*. In fact, he called these small local governments and their constitutions the true 'key' to American greatness.

"The amazing thing is how similar all these little-town

constitutions were. They were created all up and down the American coastline, from Georgia to Massachusetts, and north into what is now Canada. Seventy-five of these township constitutions are collected and discussed in one book, *Colonial Origins of the American Constitution.*

"Anyway, nearly all of the town governments were structured with the decision-making authority lodged in the adult town members voting in a weekly town meeting. This group had full legislative authority, and it voted to appoint mayor, judge, sheriff, and other executive and judicial officers to run the affairs of the people.

"All authorities had to report to this group of all citizens, which could fire them or change their responsibilities as needed. In some towns, any citizen who didn't attend the weekly meeting was fined. They took the participation of citizens very seriously."

Wendell looked around to see if everyone was still interested. "Keep going," Monte urged.

"Okay. As the nation grew, and larger groups developed into colonies and eventually states, the state governments wrote their constitutions in ways that built directly on the authority of these local systems. When the Framers wrote the U.S. Constitution, they knowingly structured it on the foundation of these local town meetings and expected weekly, active, citizen participation to continue."

Wendell fished the iPad out of his briefcase and said, "Here is one of the things Tocqueville said about it . . ." He quickly scanned his bookmarks and pushed a key. "The political existence of the majority of European nations commenced at the national level and then moved downward," he summarized. "Tocqueville then says, 'In America, on the other hand, it may be said that the township was organized before the county, the county before the state, and the state before the Union.'"

"So, the citizens were officially and fully involved? All of them?" David asked. "They participated every week in a government meeting, where important issues were debated and voted on?

No wonder they were supercitizens. They were raised reading and absorbing this stuff, and then they spent their adult lives totally involved in governance?"

"Yes," Wendell said. "When it came time to elect big-city, county, state, and national representatives, the American people knew the leaders they were voting for up close and personal. They all knew the issues intricately, had read what the great political thinkers of history wrote about them, and knew what policies had been tried and how well they worked—or didn't work.

"And as the settlers moved west, they established the same system in the new towns clear across the continent. This was the American governance system, and it was all based on real and active citizen participation."

Monte spoke up: "Actually, Kami mentioned something about this at our San Diego meeting, but I didn't realize how deep this goes. So, when it came time for the Constitutional Convention, the Framers knew this was the local system and they wrote the Constitution with the knowledge that the people were this thoroughly involved and would keep a very close eye on everything the government did.

"Then, as the nation grew and this local system was changed, the people stopped participating so closely."

"And the people began leaving the future of the nation, its laws, and its policies to their elected officials," Spence said. "Naturally, the result was that power shifted from the people to the state and eventually from the state to the federal level. And from the people to the wealthy, also."

"Excellent," Kami said, and wrote *Townships* on the whiteboard. "Now, if we could go back in time and tell the Framers that the local system would be lost unless they wrote it into the Constitution, what would we tell them to write? How would we suggest that they amend the Constitution to address this?"

"Actually," David said, "I have an idea. I have a proposed

government system I wrote while I was brainstorming about solutions to this project after San Diego. I was reading a business book, *The 48 Laws of Power*, by Robert Greene, and something about our modern lack of business involvement in local government made me think. I mean, I pay a great deal in taxes each year, but in truth, I really don't even know my local, county, or state government leaders—not to mention federal.

"In frustration, I wrote out a plan of how to remedy this. I made copies of the proposal for everyone, and I was going to bring them in later today. But if we take a quick break I'll get them from my room and we can talk about them right now. What do you think?" David asked the group.

"Let's do it," Luke immediately said.

27

"Should we let Group 2 know what David's team is doing, Mr. President? I mean, they're pursuing exactly the same thing."

James thought about it for a moment. "No, Josh. Let's see what they come up with on their own."

Shall we get started?" Kami announced, and the various conversations taking place around the room went quiet.

Kami turned to David, who passed copies of his notes around the table.

"This is rough," David admitted, "because I'm still working out the nuances. But I think it can get us started. It is broken into twenty-eight small proposals, and together these form a major overhaul of our current government—but in a way that preserves our fundamental constitutional system and freedoms while making sure more power stays at the local level."

"We'll be the judge of that," Spence said jokingly. Everyone laughed except David, who was focused on how to present his proposal.

"Hold on," Monte suggested. "I know that look on David's face." He turned to David and asked, "Is this just a proposal...or are you deeply invested in it? Is this meeting going to turn into you defending each point and the rest of us poking holes in it, or are we going to all do this in a calm, casual way?"

David knew Monte had a point, so he relaxed and grinned. "You know me too well, Monte. Okay, I'll chill out and try not to get caught up in the pride of ownership. In fact, Kami, could you lead us through this proposal? I'll approach it critically along with everyone else and see if it stands up to scrutiny."

"Excellent," Spence said. "I've learned from years in the courtroom to watch the body language of each person, and your body language said that you were gearing up to win a heated debate. I like your more relaxed posture now."

"Okay," Kami began. "Item 1: Money is backed by 100 percent gold standard—"

David interrupted, "This kills many fraudulent activities that always initiate the Five Laws of Decline."

"Really?" Spence asked without letting David finish. "We're going to start the proposal with that? How does that get business leaders more involved as citizens?"

Everyone looked at David. "Well, without going back to the gold standard to support our currency, the government will always print money to serve itself, thus causing inflation and hurting business. I think business leaders understand this better than most, actually."

"It will never pass in Congress or anywhere else," Spence argued.

"Wait," Luke interrupted. "We promised not to focus on initial problems but rather on opportunities. What is the opportunity created by this proposal?"

"Let me answer the question, please," Spence responded. "This whole exercise of going through David's proposal is to focus on the opportunity. And if we don't discuss each point as we go, the whole thing will waste our time, won't it?"

"That's an excellent point," Monte said. "We need to talk frankly about the proposal."

"This is political suicide," Spence reiterated. "The way Washington works—"

"But Republican and Democrat is the wrong dichotomy," David interrupted.

Spence looked surprised, but he was intrigued by David's point. "What do you mean?" he asked.

"Well, the way Washington works is part of the problem. The party system is a major part of the problem. I'm not concerned about the Democratic or the Republican views of all this; I'm only interested in the American future. Who cares if you're Democrat or Republican if the nation goes bankrupt? Let's talk about freedom, and the principles that are most likely to bring increased freedom, and let's forget what Washington and the political parties want."

Kami jumped in: "In purely political terms, there is actually more support around the nation for this nonpartisan view than for either big political party. We want leaders from all walks of life, not from any one party."

"I don't disagree," Spence said thoughtfully. "But this approach is easier to claim than to actually apply."

"I have a thought." David got everyone's attention. "Let's read the first eight points, then discuss them as a whole. They basically go together."

Kami waited to see if anyone had a concern, then began reading:

2. Citizens and corporations write three separate tax checks to local, state, and federal government each year.
3. Four percent of your net income goes to local, 3 percent to state, and 3 percent to federal.
4. There are no loopholes or exclusions, and these are the only taxes in the nation.
5. All governments must pass a budget by the first day of each year, and if the government fails to do this or at any point spends more than the budget, all officials of that government will be put up for reelection immediately.

6. If the government needs to use debt for any reason, all officials of that government go up for reelection immediately.

7. When a reelection run is needed, the officials will remain in office until the next election, to be held twenty-five days after the need is triggered.

8. If Congress declares war, all states will reduce their budgets from 3 percent down to 1 percent of the tax revenues, and the extra 2 percent will go to the federal government to fund the war. A majority of states must vote for this to occur and to continue the war. If the cost of winning the war exceeds this additional money, the local government will do the same thing, and it must be supported by a vote of the majority of local governments in the nation. If still more money is needed, a majority of states may vote to borrow money and allow future state taxes to pay for it (without raising the 3 percent).

"Whoa! This is terrible," Spence exclaimed. "How can we possibly hope to compete with the rising power of China and other nations under such a system? And we'll have to end so many key government programs that this will literally gut our nation. I think this brand of nonpartisanship will have both parties against you!"

"Actually, I think we should take the time to think this through," David responded. "I've given a lot of thought to this proposal, and I think it will stand up to deeper analysis. If we do discover any flaws, we certainly wouldn't want to adopt them. But the real question is this: what parts of it do we really need?"

"I agree," Wendell said. "David is a top expert on the Five Laws of Decline and using them to bring about successful turnarounds. This proposal is unique and profound, so far. Let's look for how it might really help, and I think we'll find some very important principles we can use—even if there are some things we don't want."

"I think that's the right approach," Luke said. "Not: will every single detail in the proposal work? That's not our point. We should simply ask if any of the points would work! If they will, we need them."

"Is there anything in these first eight points that would keep the 10 percent actively involved as supercitizens?" Kami asked the group.

"I really like the gold standard," Monte said. "I think it would increase the general wealth of the nation and keep more people in a position where they can afford to be actively involved citizens. I don't think most people know how significant this is.

"When a government prints its own money, then inflates it by printing more, the masses are the ones who lose out. The wealthy don't store most of their wealth in currency, they put it in gold or land or stock, so when inflation makes fuel, food, clothes, rent, and everything else more expensive, the poor suffer even more.

"The divide between the rich and poor widens, and the regular people have less economic opportunity. A class system solidifies, jobs become scarce, and more power shifts to Washington and Wall Street. The gold standard stops a lot of that."

"Actually, it's the gold and silver standard," Luke mentioned. "Every successful system using a gold standard allows for both silver and gold to be used as currency."

"This shift back to the gold standard might not pass Congress, like Spence said," Kami spoke slowly, "but if the 10 percent are fully engaged they will understand finance and this could change."

"I actually like nearly all of this proposal, so far," Wendell said. "The proposed tax percentages of 4, 3, and 3 percent to local, state, and federal has merit. Even if we use higher percentages, or give 4 to state and 3 to local, the whole idea is seriously worth considering.

"Also," he continued, "the reelection when government officials fail to do their job or start overspending or borrowing too much has at least two consequences. First, officials will be loath to put themselves back into an election cycle by being unwise with the people's money; and second, the citizens will know immediately when the Constitution is broken, and they'll have to take action at the voting booth within the month. That will get a lot more regular people closely involved.

"On the other hand, I'm not a fan of election recall, because it leads to a mob mentality in the voting public. If our so-called supercitizens become too involved, meaning that they call for a new election every time they dislike what some governmental official does, freedom will suffer just as much or more than it already has."

Wendell looked up. "But at this local level, the more involvement the better, right? Or what if instead of an immediate reelection, spending beyond the budget simply came out of the officials' pay? Or perhaps there is some other way to get the same result without the negative side effects?"

28

"Josh, make sure the two groups don't collaborate. We need to see what they'll come up with separately."

"Yes, Mr. President."

I think we should look at this from the big picture," David said. "Would setting up the tax system this way get the 10 percent truly involved in our modern world? Would such a system of funding wars do it? That's how we need to look at these proposals.

"Look, I don't want to rewrite the Constitution. I love the Constitution. It is the greatest freedom document in history. But clearly it isn't working as well we need it to anymore. It's working better than anything else, for sure, and I wouldn't change it unless we knew we had something better.

"But if the original Framers assumed a certain kind of local government and the type of citizens this created, and we've lost that part of it, we aren't so much restructuring the Constitution as rebuilding it on its original foundations."

"I have concerns about how war is declared in this proposal," Wendell said.

Spence raised his hand and Kami called on him. "I think we should first read through the next eight items in the proposal," he said. "We're trying to comment on something we don't yet really understand."

"Good idea," Amy added, "and as we read on, let's look for any items that we think would really overcome the Laws of Decline."

Kami picked up her copy of the proposal and read:

9. The Supreme Court is the high court and final arbiter of any case, but its decisions do not set any precedent at all.

10. Senators will be appointed by each state legislature, not by the popular vote of the people in that state.

11. Each local area will elect a mayor to oversee the business of the local government.

12. The mayor shall be elected by a majority vote of all citizens in the locale. In cities, a city mayor may be elected by the populace, but the city mayor will not take the place of the local mayors.

Spence spoke up: "That way, a current city like Milwaukee or Cincinnati won't have to change its whole system. It will still have a city mayor, but it will also now have a whole bunch of small local systems, each with its own local mayor, right?"

"Yes." David nodded. Kami started reading again:

13. Each local government will elect a board of ten members to review the decisions of the mayor. This board will have no power to do anything except veto proposals by the mayor.

14. If the board vote supports a mayoral proposal instead of vetoing it, the proposal will be voted on by the whole town in the next monthly town meeting. Each locale will hold a town meeting each month.

15. The ten board members will be elected each year by a weighted tax vote. This vote will include all citizens of the local government, and each citizen will have at least one vote. A citizen will be given an additional vote for every $1,000 he or she paid in taxes the previous year. Each voter

can cast his or her votes for up to three board members, but no more than three. Persons who want to voluntarily pay more than the 10 percent tax may do so and receive additional votes in this weighted election.

16. The major roles of the mayor will be to take care of all needed business within the locale while staying within the budget, and to keep the federal and state governments from encroaching on the powers of the local government.

Kami stopped reading and looked up at the group.

"Well, I'll say one thing," Spence said, "you certainly are thinking out of the box."

"But is there anything you like, Senator?" Luke directed his question at Spence.

"Actually, there is. I don't like the proposed changes to the Supreme Court or the way senators are elected, but I do think the local angle has a lot of merit. I'll have to give more thought to the weighted-vote idea, but I think the rest of it could effectively pull in the involvement of a lot more regular citizens."

"I agree," Wendell said, "though I do like the senatorial and Supreme Court changes. The change to local government has a lot of merit. The way the board serves only as a veto board for proposals is interesting and excellent—"

Monte interrupted: "The weighted vote is genius! The whole local government structure gets many more citizens actively involved, and the weighted vote incentivizes business leaders to participate at much higher levels. But the fact that they can only vote for three possible board members means that one rich person can't appoint the whole board."

"I have one concern about the board of ten," Wendell said. "When the American Revolution came, the Americans were different from most British colonies because American colonies had their own parliaments. The British usually didn't allow this, but the

Americans really wanted them, and the British allowed them with the stipulation that the American parliaments could suggest things but really had no power without the agreement of the British Parliament.

"But when things got so bad that the various colonies felt the need to break from Britain, they ignored the fact that most of their parliaments had no actual legal power and just acted as if they did. They voted for taxes, collected them, raised militias, and basically just behaved as if they had legal power."

"That's how many business boards actually work as well," Luke said.

"Except for one thing," David added. "On most business boards, the members are closely invested and interested, so they take immediate action if it is needed. That's precisely what we need the 10 percent to do for America."

Wendell nodded. "Throughout history, political bodies nearly always try to increase their power without waiting for their constitutions to change. So, in this proposal, I think we can pretty much expect the local boards to eventually ignore the fact that they are only supposed to negate things and they'll start making proposals, voting, and trying to enforce things."

"But every vote they take has to be voted on by the whole citizenry," Monte pointed out.

"I was just getting there," Wendell said. "The natural division between the mayor and the board of ten will make it hard to fool the people. These groups will probably argue a lot. But even if they do agree on something, the whole citizenry will have to vote on it.

"To make sure this happens, the monthly town meeting of all citizens should appoint its own leaders to attend board meetings and report on all their votes to the whole town. They shouldn't leave it to the mayor or board to tell the monthly town meeting what they voted on. And all town and board meetings should be open to the public, not closed.

"I know this is a little complex," Wendell apologized, "but that's how free people need to think."

"That's a good addition," David said, as he took notes on his handout.

Luke shook his head in amazement, and Michelle noticed his reaction.

"What are you thinking, Luke?" she asked.

"Well," he said, as everyone shifted their attention in his direction, "I just want to know who created the group in this room right now. Seriously, what kind of people wake up one day and think, *Hey, let's meet at a top ski resort and fix America's problems, and while we're at it let's get our citizenry and business leaders to read great classics and argue about whether city councils or local boards are best?* I mean, really! This whole retreat is quite a surprise."

"It makes sense for Wendell to be here, or even me," Spence said, nodding. "After all, we both make our living dealing with such issues. But as for the rest of you, I agree with Luke. This is remarkable."

"It's a microcosm of exactly what we're trying to see happen across the nation, isn't it?" Marcus replied.

Monte disagreed, saying, "Actually, I think quite a few populist groups and meetings discuss a lot of similar ideas. Give them credit—"

"Also political meetings of various kinds," Spence said, "but still, this is something unique. It really is. I experienced similar discussions in political science courses in college, and a little bit in law school and even policy meetings run by think tanks, but to have committed business leaders initiating something at this level? Like I said, it's remarkable—at least in my experience."

"I have some disagreements, too," Marcus proclaimed. "If I shake my head, will somebody ask me what I'm thinking... please?"

After a few people chuckled, Amy asked in mock fascination, "Marcus, what are you thinking? Will you *please* share it with us?"

"Well, if you insist. I was thinking that it's time to break for the afternoon and hit the hot tub while the sun is high. I mean, this place is gorgeous! We can't spend all of our time indoors...."

29

"Excellent group of people," James said.
"Yes, Mr. President. They are an interesting mix."

M arcus was the first to reach the hot tub, and Wendell, Monte, and Kami came along shortly thereafter.

"This view is incredible!" Monte exclaimed.

Everyone nodded emphatically.

Kami held up her wrist and showed everyone her Tommy Bahama watch. "I just love this watch," she said. "It seems to me to have a soul, a special message to the world, something like, *Relax! Stop taking yourself so seriously. Just relax!*"

Marcus knew when he was being mocked, so he started to respond: "Now, wait just a—"

"I've been worried about something all day," Wendell interrupted. "It just keeps bugging me."

"What is it?" Kami asked.

"Well, it's a widespread leadership principle that people buy into a leader first, then into the vision. For example, without George Washington, the Declaration of Independence wouldn't have had the same force, the war would probably have been lost, and the Constitutional Convention may well have failed. Leader first... then vision."

"And you're concerned that we're focusing on the vision of

American turnaround without having a political leader?" Monte said. "That's a good point."

"But isn't that kind of thinking the real problem?" asked Kami. "We keep hoping that electing the right political candidates will fix things, but it just doesn't work. The 10 percent aren't doing their job, and until they do decline will continue. After each election, those whose candidate won truly think that things will change, but they don't—not really. Not in the big ways. The problems continue without real change coming from Washington.

"We don't need a leader, we need hundreds of thousands of leaders. If we get them on board, the nation will buy into them— then to the vision of better citizenship."

"Agreed," Wendell said, "but can we get thousands of leaders without a Washington or a Jefferson to show the way?"

"Maybe not." Monte was neck deep in the hot, soothing water. "But let's look at it from a different angle. There are thousands of leaders of business organizations that already provide this kind of leadership for their groups. CEOs, company presidents and executives, professionals, multilevel and network marketing leaders, and others. They are already leading. If they buy in, they'll help those they lead do the same. Those are our leaders."

Kami nodded. "Let's not forget journalists, teachers, and entertainers. And I think there are a lot of government officials who fit this category and got involved in politics precisely because they wanted to lead in this way."

"That reminds me of something we talked about in San Diego," said Monte. "Mothers and fathers are naturally this kind of leader, if they realize how important citizenship is. I think many, maybe even most, committed parents would lead this way if they thought of it and knew how."

Marcus chimed in, "Seth Godin wrote about the emergence of many new-style tribes in our modern world, and Malcolm Gladwell teaches that our society is made up of unofficial connectors and mavens who use the Internet and personal relationships to spread important information. These online tribal thought leaders who already exist are part of the 10 percent, whether they know it or not."

David joined them in the hot tub.

"We just need to get the idea of such leadership into their minds," Kami said excitedly. "In the Founders' day it was done through pamphlets. Dozens of leaders all over the thirteen colonies wrote their ideas on freedom in pamphlets and distributed them around the nation. Books were expensive, and controlled by big publishers, most of which were owned by British companies. In our day, we just need to find the equivalent of their pamphlets."

"That's obviously the Internet," Marcus said.

Monte shook his head slowly. "I'm not so sure. The Internet is a great way for the leaders to reach their tribes, but it may not be all that helpful in reaching the leaders. Most people have a list of favorite online sites, and they don't spend much time finding new ideas in other places. For many people, the Internet has become extremely segregated into small, opinionated groups. I think we'll need another way to reach the leaders."

"Luke is amazing, isn't he?" Wendell asked nobody in particular.

Everyone nodded. "The energy in the room was palpable when he started talking," Kami said.

Wendell had an important point to make. "He manages to do his investing in a powerful way that makes a huge difference, by going under the radar and just selecting one business at a time, showing up, and asking for a job or to volunteer. Maybe our way of reaching the 10 percent leaders will be an off-the-radar strategy."

"Like what?" Monte inquired.

"I'm not sure."

"I have an idea," Kami said. "It says in *The Tipping Point* that big changes come from surprisingly small things. In fact, that's the whole point of 10 percent swaying the whole populace. Add that to Richard Weaver's classic book *Ideas Have Consequences*, and we have the rule that simple, powerful ideas can have huge influence."

"Like when the idea of freedom swept the founding generation," Wendell added.

Kami continued, "Well, such great ideas are adopted first by what business writer Geoffrey Moore calls Innovators, and then by Early Adopters. Moore's books are mostly about how to grow your business market beyond the Early Adopters to the Mainstream, which is where the profits increase.

"But in finding the 10 percent leaders, we don't have to go Mainstream. The government Innovators are already involved in closely overseeing government, but there are only a few of them. The Early Adopters may be our 10 percent."

"So we just have to understand what the Early Adopters want," Monte said, "and help them realize how much their leadership is needed."

"That's easy to say but hard to do," Marcus warned. "High-tech companies are my specialty, and the Early Adopters are the focus of tech start-ups. The thing is, Innovators like a product, service, or idea because it is cutting-edge. Period. And the Mainstream likes usability at a good price and value supported by excellent service.

"But the Early Adopters are a different story. They like something because it's cool. They like to show it to their friends, and they value the quality of an item. Usually, when a product, service, or idea spreads to the Mainstream, it loses some quality in the name of availability—"

Kami interrupted. "Like the individualized one-room school being replaced by large conveyor-belt schools. More people get educated, but the quality can suffer."

"The same thing sometimes happens when a business grows a lot," Marcus continued. "Quality and individualization are often sacrificed for standardization and profit."

Kami nodded. "But the key point is that Early Adopters value a product or idea that is both high-quality and cool, right?"

"Precisely," Marcus affirmed.

"I see where you're going, Kami," Wendell said. "How can spending an hour or more a day studying what the government is doing be made cool?"

Everyone pondered the question.

Finally, Wendell stood up and toweled off. Then he turned to the group and said, "An under-the-radar strategy to make it cool to be true citizen-leaders. Wouldn't that be a shift—"

"A LeaderShift!" Monte suddenly exclaimed.

30

"But, Mr. President, it really wasn't a good idea for the Constitutional Convention to start writing articles about local government. That had to be left to the people."

"Well, that may be true, Josh, but he's right. We did just assume that local government would always be around. We didn't realize the full extent to which our local system truly trained leaders, and when we lost that leadership training our nation began to suffer. I wish David had been there to teach us the Five Laws. I don't care if it's presumptuous. It also happens to be true!"

"But then, wouldn't they have just changed that, too, when they passed the Seventeenth Amendment, Mr. President?"

"That's a good point." James stroked his chin. "But they didn't. And such a change now could make all the difference."

W hat's a LeaderShift?" Luke asked as the participants were returning to the conference room. "I heard Monte and Wendell discussing it at dinner. Does it apply to this evening's session?"

"I think so," Monte said. "It really describes exactly where we are right now in modern business."

"Let's talk about it," David said, as everyone took their seats around the table.

"It fits right in with David's proposal, especially the parts about local government." Kami turned to Wendell. "Maybe you should tell the whole group what we talked about with those at our dinner table..."

Wendell nodded. "The earliest leaders were warriors, and when our ancestors changed from a nomadic to an agrarian society, humanity experienced a LeaderShift from warriors as the top leaders to landowners as the main leaders. The next LeaderShift occurred when professionals like doctors and lawyers became the main town and societal leaders, and then later, another LeaderShift put executives and managers at the top of the leadership ladder."

"That was called the Management Revolution, and it happened in the nineteen forties, fifties, and sixties," Marcus said. "It was written about by W. Edwards Deming and William Whyte."

Wendell continued, "Then came the next LeaderShift—the Leadership Revolution, led by thinkers from Dale Carnegie and Buckminster Fuller to Warren Bennis, Peter Drucker, and Stephen Covey, among others."

"Each time a LeaderShift occurs," Kami said, "a whole new level of leadership develops, and the definition of what it means to be a good leader evolves."

"For example"—Marcus was intensely interested—"effective management was all about doing things right, then the LeaderShift changed things to a focus on doing the right things. But leaders doing the right things were also expected to do things right. So each LeaderShift tends to increase the quality of leadership in society."

Monte added, "The whole point of this is that we are now experiencing another LeaderShift. This time the added focus is that leaders can't just do the right things for the organizations they lead, they also must do the right things for the freedom and prosperity of the nation."

"That's so cool!" Marcus said enthusiastically.

Wendell spoke slowly. "The challenge is to make it seem 'cool' to the Early Adopters in society, since they make up many of the 10 percent leaders."

Luke leaned forward in his chair and said intensely, "I spend most of my time finding Innovators and Early Adopters and helping them succeed. To me, this is a profound idea. And it's an idea whose time has come."

"Can we get back to the proposal?" suggested Spence. "I can hardly wait to see what else David is proposing."

"I'll read it," Kami said:

17. State governors are elected by a majority vote of local mayors within the state.
18. Each governor must have served as a local mayor.
19. Governors play two roles: (1) maintain the budget and services within the state, and (2) ensure that the federal government doesn't encroach on the powers of the state.
20. A majority of local mayors within a state can veto any law passed by the state government and/or any policy adopted by the governor.
21. The town meeting will annually elect, by majority vote, a justice of the peace to oversee judicial disputes within the town.
22. The justice of the peace may be removed in a town meeting by a two-thirds vote of the town.
23. All state and federal government meetings are open to the public and broadcast on cable television. There are no closed hearings or meetings in government except military meetings.
24. State and county courts oversee all disputes between localities and appeals of decisions from justices of the peace.
25. The president shall be elected by a majority vote of the state governors.
26. The president must have served as a state governor.
27. The Constitution may be amended by a two-thirds vote of Congress and two-thirds of the states and two-thirds of the local governments.

28. Unless changed by these twenty-eight points, the U.S. Constitution will remain in force as is, and states shall change their constitutions as needed to meet these alterations.

"That's the proposal," Kami concluded.

Spence spoke up immediately. "Before we talk about the pros and cons of individual items, I want to make a point. I think the whole thing is way too long to be as effective as we hope. We should choose a few of the items, no more than ten or so, and suggest them to America's business leaders. A list this long is going to get lost, but a smaller, more focused list will be much stickier."

"I agree," Marcus said. "A shorter list is more cool, which will appeal to more people."

David nodded. "It's like Patrick Henry's Seven Resolutions, which so effectively swayed those who heard him. More of the proposal can be added later, but we need to identify and promote those that will most effectively capture the imagination of the 10 percent."

"How are we going to do that?" Luke asked. "I can help fund this project, and I have some colleagues who will participate. Spence, can your contacts in Washington help David spread his message of Seven Resolutions or something similar?"

"Yes," said Spence, nodding. "Once we narrow down the exact proposal, we can get them heard in the right places. But we still haven't narrowed this down to the right resolutions. They need to be beyond partisan politics, and they need to effectively get the top business leaders involved in overseeing government."

"Wait," Kami said. "Aren't we going in the wrong direction? Why do we want this to be heard in Washington? Don't we want to focus on business leaders instead?"

Luke jumped in: "But the best way to get them involved is to make it part of their passion and profit at the same time. And the most effective thing we've come up with is to get business and other leaders more actively involved at the local level. This means getting

Washington and the states to adopt a new model where local citizens are officially in government."

"That's such a big objective...maybe too big," Wendell warned.

"That's very possible," Luke retorted, "but we shouldn't shy away from the idea just because it's hard. We should figure out what would keep regular citizens, at least 10 percent of them, actively participating in government leadership, and then we should make it happen. If we fail, at the very least we'll promote the ideas more widely. And if we don't even try, well, we fail by fiat."

"Big things are done by people who do what seemed impossible before they did it," Michelle said.

"Here's the big question." Luke turned to David. "Which five or seven points will effectively engage the 10 percent if they are adopted, in a way that the decline caused by the Five Laws will be reversed? Whatever they are, we need to get the nation to understand and adopt them. It will be hard, yes. Incredibly hard. So let's get started."

PART IV

31

"I think you need to see this, Mr. President."

"Group 1 or Group 2?" James asked.

"Actually, both..." Josh let the words hang in the air.

James put down the book and hurried up the hall.

Senator Cecil Markham Huntington laid down the newspaper and leaned back in his leather chair. "You have to admit they're gaining a surprising level of support. Where did they come from, Tom?" he asked.

Thomas Keynes was the heir to the huge Keynes fortune and chairman of a Wall Street investment conglomerate, as well as the head of several foundations. "My investigators say they are well funded by Luke DiCastro, the oil billionaire and investor, and of course everyone knows Senator Spencer Boardman. But at the center of the group is David Mersher, the turnaround specialist. The rest are following David's lead."

"It's strange that Spence is working with them." Senator Huntington shook his head. "He's done so much for globalism. Why is he promoting this localism thing?"

Keynes sighed. "They've done a remarkable job of making this a bipartisan issue. *It's not about Democrats or Republicans at all—it's about getting business leaders and other citizens more involved in leading the nation.* They're appealing to anyone who is tired of seeing

Washington fiddle while the nation burns, so to speak. They've got a lot of support from people of both parties as well as independents.

"They only need two more states to ratify their proposed amendment and we'll have the first constitutional convention since the founding. But I think the bigger danger is if David's words to the joint committee next week will convince a few more congressmen to vote for the amendment. They're so close to two-thirds in both houses..."

"Not to mention the frustrating number of calls we are all getting from citizens. It's another jam-the-phone-lines thing. We can ignore it, but some legislators will inevitably cave to public pressure."

"Cecil, what's it going to take to stop it?"

"The committee hearing? Or the vote to propose the amendment?"

"Both."

"Well, they've got a long road ahead. They've got to do well in the hearing, well enough to swing at least thirty-one votes in the House and four in the Senate. That's not impossible, but it's not going to be easy for them.

"Then, even if that works, they've got to push through the vote. Spence knows the inside track on this, so they have a chance there. But with the right pressure from big donors..."

"I'll handle that," Keynes said.

"Excellent. But here's the real challenge. Even if they sway the votes in the hearings and are able to maintain them through the actual vote, getting the amendment to pass in three-fourths of the states is going to be a huge problem. We'll use everything we have to oppose it. I really don't think they will get this done."

"Do I need to start organizing opposition in all the states?" Keynes asked.

The senator shook his head curtly. "I think that's premature, but I'll keep a close eye it."

"So will I." Keynes paused. Then he asked, "What about shutting down the committee hearing somehow?"

"We thought of that," Senator Huntington said. "But they would just push for a reschedule. The best thing is for them to have their hearing and then just lose the vote. That's where my colleagues and I will put all our energy."

"Who else should we get involved?" Keynes asked.

The two men leaned forward to look at the long list of names, organizations, and companies on the senator's desk.

32

"Do you think Thomas will be interested? He's been so busy the last few decades with the technological projects. I just don't know if he'll appreciate a shift back to the governmental department. He didn't enjoy it that much the first time around. Have you asked him?"

"No, sir, I haven't. But we need him. I'll have to make the case for it, and make it compelling enough that he can't say no."

The tall man stroked his chin while he thought. Then, with a short nod, he said, "Good luck, James. I agree that we could really use his keen insight." Then he chuckled. "You redheads and your insight," he added affectionately.

Yes, I've done an extensive review of their proposal, and I think we're in trouble," Dr. Marcellus Connor said.

When nobody responded, he continued, "As a Nobel Laureate in economics, I analyze many proposals, but this one cuts right to the marrow of our system."

"Well," Senator Huntington said, "that's why we called you in. Let's do damage control. How bad is it?"

"I assume we're talking about the regular fee, is that correct, Mr. Keynes?"

"Yes," Keynes responded smoothly. "Of course."

"Very well." Connor took a deep breath and glanced at his

notebook. "I've taken a long list of notes, and I'll go through them one by one." He paused, then began, "The bad news is that David Mersher is right about his Nine Resolves Amendment choking off the government use of what he refers to as 'Other People's Money' or 'OPM.' This proposal does exactly that.

"As you know, OPM is at the crux of the upper crust's ability to lead society. Unless the right people are managing the economy, the market will crassly choose the wrong priorities for the nation's money.

"John Maynard Keynes understood this." Connor turned to Keynes and asked, "Are you any relation?" When Keynes merely smiled, Connor continued, "He taught that in our modern free-market nations the best way to get socialist goals and a more fair distribution of resources would be to use markets to support socialist aims."

Connor paused. "I know that of course neither of you wants to be pinned with the *socialist* label, so let's use a different word here: *fairness*.

"The best way to get fairness, Keynes wrote, would be for big business to overtake small business. Most people don't understand what is happening when this occurs, just like most people don't understand the real differences between paper and gold money, but the upper crust will know exactly what is going on. Small businesses, you see, tend to operate with the goals of profit along with their central corporate mission.

"In contrast, big business tends to put mission behind it and focuses on profit—especially for their shareholders. But, as Keynes brilliantly pointed out, some companies become so big that they start caring more about public relations than market success. When they reach this point, they are natural supporters of fairness rather than capitalism. They'll use their influence and resources to promote the ideals of socialism—or rather, *fairness*—throughout society.

"Keynes mentioned big utility and industrial companies as examples of this, but in our day there are hundreds of corporations in many nations that fit this definition. As you know, these big businesses collaborate with government to redistribute the profits from small and medium-size businesses and individual taxpayers to fund most government projects.

"What is unique about David Mersher's proposal is that it would put an end to this system. It's as if he saw precisely what makes the current system work. If his proposal passes, the upper crust will be far less able to direct the bulk of the nation's spending. When the income tax amendment was adopted in 1913, for example, the highest tax rate in the U.S. was only 2 percent. But, as the old saying goes, 'Let the camel's nose inside your tent, and pretty soon the whole camel is lounging in your bed.'"

"I remember that proverb a little differently," Senator Huntington said drily.

"In any case," Dr. Connor continued, "the upper crust was able to slowly increase this percentage until we now manage most of the nation's discretionary funds. Under David Mersher's plan, control over these resources would be given to local and state decision makers, and we would need to devise a new method for getting the money back under our management."

"That would be a disaster," Keynes said slowly. "Not insurmountable, but not desirable, either."

"Very true," said Connor. "But that's just the bad news. The worse news is that if this passes, we won't be able to use government regulation to ensure monopoly prices for the really big companies. Nor will we be able to use military might so easily to protect some of our global interests—"

"You think it's easy to get military support?" the senator interrupted. "You should see how much it takes to drum up enough votes for—"

"But it will become much more difficult if this plan passes,"

Connor said firmly. "*Much* more difficult. Also, if it passes there will be no unchecked powers. The local governments will be able to check the loopholes we've used for the past century, from treaties and court redefinitions to printing currency. And the ridiculous gold standard part of the plan will totally remake our economic system—the upper crust will be weakened for at least a generation."

"So it's bad," Keynes said. "Well, we knew that already. The only answer is to shut it down."

Connor raised a finger. "Actually, I really haven't told you the worst part yet. I've shared the bad news, and the worse news, but not yet the very worst."

Keynes was getting slightly annoyed with the economist's flair for the dramatic, but he didn't show it. Both men simply looked at Connor, so he continued:

"The 10 percent tax limit means that there will be no import taxes, and as former senator Spencer Boardman keeps repeating to the media, China is growing by adopting free enterprise at the same time that North America is struggling because it is moving away from free enterprise."

Connor thought he had made his point, but the other two men were obviously still waiting for the punch line. "What this means," he said, slipping into his lecture voice, "is that the global agenda may be seriously compromised. Local and state leaders are going to make decisions for the interests of their people—not for global fairness.

"It's the opposite of Keynes's point. If more power is retained at the lower levels of government, regardless of whether conservatives or progressives are in office, the macroeffect will be more government policy that promotes individual prosperity and individual freedom rather than long-term global social programs. It will reverse our most important gains over the past century."

Both men now clearly got it, but their responses were diametrically different. "That's a serious problem," Senator Huntington exclaimed angrily.

Thomas Keynes was smiling widely. "To the contrary," he mused. Then, almost to himself, he said, "Finally, a worthy opponent. At least a few should come along every generation, but it's been sparse lately."

After a moment's pause, he leaned backed and sighed happily. "This is going to be very enjoyable."

Senator Huntington and Dr. Connor looked at each other, partly in surprise but mostly with concern.

"What do you mean, exactly?" Connor asked.

"It's not really important." Keynes changed the subject. "So, Doctor, is that all?"

"Well, no. I could of course go into more detail about any of the—"

"Not now," Keynes said. "Write it in your report. Is there anything else that goes beyond details? Anything truly significant that stands out?"

Connor scanned through his notes. "Oh, yes," he said. "Here's one. The first big challenge the American upper crust faced when the U.S. Constitution was ratified was how to overcome the problem of the Electoral College. Many Americans were excited about the Electoral College, but the leadership in New York, where most of the upper crust resided, realized that—"

"Can we get right to the point?" Keynes asked, as he checked his watch.

"Yes, of course," Dr. Connor said. "The operating principle of the masses, as articulated by Lord Acton, is that power corrupts. In contrast, the operating directive of the upper crust is that it is the nature of power to centralize, and once it is centralized in one place the nature of power is to expand its control as far as possible.

"So the Framers, using the idea that power corrupts, put many checks, balances, and limits on government. The upper crust, who understood the centralizing nature of power, went to work getting power amassed in one place so they could have as much influence as possible on the seat of power. The obvious place to centralize power was the federal government, particularly in either the presidency or the Supreme Court.

"Under the original Electoral College, voters in each state elected people they knew and trusted to go to a special meeting, nominate candidates for president, interview the candidates, and decide who would be the best president. Most of those appointed to the Electoral College in the early years of America were business leaders, not government types, which is exactly what Mersher and his people want.

"In fact, as you probably know, originally nobody actually ran for the office of president, and those who wanted to run were deemed too ambitious and therefore unfit by the members of the Electoral College. The upper crust saw how problematic this system was, because the two elections held this way gave us George Washington, who refused to centralize power.

"They realized that such a system would never give us a President Alexander Hamilton, for example. Or even a President Aaron Burr. It would probably have continued like this, but the upper crust saw where this was headed and influenced immediate change.

"Specifically, they used their wealth and influence to push for political parties, thus breaking up the democratic power of the Electoral College. By having the candidates come from parties, the upper crust was able to again sway elections by their influence in the media, party leadership, and academia."

Senator Huntington gasped: "Are you saying that the Nine Resolves will weaken the party system?"

"No, worse. I'm saying that it will end the party system as we know it," Dr. Connor affirmed. "No upper crust, no matter how well-funded, can sway the parties in hundreds of thousands of township votes each month.

"In fact, each little local area will have its own upper crust, made up mostly of business leaders, and they will tend to compete with each other at the state and national levels. We won't have to just influence the two big parties and Washington anymore. We'll have to try to sway many thousands of elections each year.

"Moreover, the skirmishes for funding will be less between big business and big government—which has given us significant room to tax and maneuver things to our way of running the nation. Under David Mersher's plan, the conflicts will be between various government officials competing with each other. The people will manage their officials, rather than the upper crust managing the people."

The smile on Thomas Keynes's face was gone.

Connor spoke slowly for effect. "In short, if the Nine Resolves go through, political parties and Washington will decline, and power will center in the local governments, and even more in local business leaders."

"And then their power will seek to expand..." Senator Huntington let his words trail off.

Keynes took the phone from his vest and dialed a number, then he stood and walked out of the room. As he opened the door, the other men heard him say, "Bonnie, please have Ronald call our media CEOs like we discussed, and get me Barbra Gibson on the phone immediately..."

33

"How did Group 2 know to focus on the local leadership system?"

"We're not sure, Mr. President. I reviewed all the logs, and there was no crossover between the two groups. Group 2 studied the recordings between 1789 and 1913 and pinpointed the loss of local leadership involvement as the biggest problem. I knew you'd ask about this, so I've pored over the reports from both groups: Group 2 didn't get it from Group 1."

"Interesting..." James stared at the large screen.

M r. Mersher, you may proceed to reread your Nine Resolves of the proposed amendment for the record," Chairperson Gibson announced.

David smiled and read:

1. All cities and local areas in the United States shall be divided into townships made up of no less than eight hundred voting citizens and no more than twelve hundred voting citizens.

"I'm going to interrupt you right there," Chairperson Gibson said. Then she sighed and leaned back in her chair. "These hearings can be tedious, and we've all read your Nine Resolves. Before you go through them again, answer this question: Why are you doing this? Why does the nation need such a sweeping change, and how can we know that it will even work? What do you really want to accomplish with all of this?"

"I want the people to get involved in the government, especially at the local level. Our nation faces so many problems, and until—"

"We're aware of the problems," Chairperson Gibson interrupted again. "We deal with them every day. But what makes you think your Resolves will fix anything? Our democracy works slowly, and it is far from perfect, but what makes you think your plan can do better? Have you considered that this entire endeavor might be a huge waste of our time?"

David smiled. He felt relaxed, and he was enjoying this, even though the chair wasn't giving him the normal time to speak. After the many hours of practice sessions he had done with Spence, Wendell, and Kami, this wasn't very hard at all. They had grilled him in every imaginable way.

"If I can have my normally allotted time to read the proposal and make my statement, I think I'll answer these questions to your satisfaction," David said pleasantly.

"Very well." Chairperson Gibson reluctantly leaned forward and spoke into the microphone. "Proceed."

"Thank you," David said. Then he read:

2. The citizens of each township shall meet once a month at a time and place of the township's own choosing, and shall by majority vote elect a mayor and whatever other officers are deemed necessary to run the business of the township. The mayor shall carry out the business of the township as determined by the town meeting. In large cities, there may be many township mayors working in addition to the city's mayor.

3. The town meeting shall also elect ten members to a township board using a weighted vote. In this weighted vote, every citizen shall have at least one vote; in addition, each citizen

will have an extra vote for every $1,000 paid in the previous year's taxes. Where a couple pays a joint tax, only one extra vote will be given for each $1,000 paid. Each voter shall vote for up to three members of the board, but for no more than three.

4. The township board of ten shall have the authority to veto any proposal of the township mayor, and this shall be the limit of the board's power. If a proposal from the mayor isn't vetoed by the board within a month, it shall be presented to the vote of the citizens at the next township meeting and pass with a majority vote.

5. The major responsibilities of the township mayor shall be to carry out township business within the allotted budget and to keep state, county, city, and/or any other higher levels of government from encroaching on the powers of the township.

6. Mayors and board members shall be elected annually. All governments must pass a budget by the first day of each year, and if the mayor and/or board members ever fail to do this, or spend beyond the budget, go into debt, or otherwise exceed their authority as outlined herein, a new election will be held within thirty days.

7. All tax law(s) will be changed to the following: henceforth every citizen will write three checks when they pay their taxes: 4 percent of their net income to the local township, 3 percent to the state government, and 3 percent to the federal government. No other taxes shall be paid.

8. If Congress declares war, all states will reduce their budgets from 3 percent down to 1 percent of the tax revenues, and the extra 2 percent will go to the federal government to fund the war. A majority of states must vote for this to occur; they must thereafter vote annually for this to continue. If the cost of winning the war exceeds this additional money, the local

government will do the same thing, and it must be supported by a vote of the majority of local governments in the nation. If still more money is needed, a majority of states may vote to borrow money and allow future state taxes to pay for it (without raising the 3 percent).

9. The nation shall adopt a gold and silver standard for all currency, with all government currency coined in gold and/or silver or redeemable for such.

"Madame Chair," Representative Collins said loudly.

"The chair recognizes the representative from Vermont," Chairperson Gibson announced.

"I move that we end this ridiculous hearing right now."

Chairperson Gibson looked around the podium to gauge the feelings of the committee.

"Let the man have his say," Representative Parker said. "Let's give everyone five minutes to ask questions, and then let's vote. I know it's a little irregular, but so is this entire proceeding."

Spence leaned over and whispered into David's ear as the committee went through its discussion of how to proceed. "You're doing great, David. Just keep your calm and let this run its course."

34

"Mr. President, there's been a development."

The tall man turned and grinned at James. "How many times do I have to tell you to call me George?"

James nodded respectfully.

"But what's the development?" Washington asked.

"Well, David's team, Group 1, and Group 2 are all working on the same thing."

"Local leadership, as we discussed?"

"Yes, sir," James said, nodding.

"And so?"

"Well, sir, I may need to, uh . . ." James searched for the right word. ". . . innovate."

The tall man smiled. "So, what's new?"

When the questions started, some of the representatives were intense and negative, others more supportive. David answered whatever questions they asked directly and without evasion. Spence had coached him that such frankness and candor would be unexpected and win him points even with those who were against the Nine Resolves.

"The rule in politics is never to answer the question you are asked," Spence had told him, "but rather to answer the question you think the person *should* have asked . . . or whatever best makes the point you want to promote. But many politicians have taken this to such an extreme that it sometimes feels like few elected officials actually answer questions. Break that pattern, and you'll make friends."

Then, almost as an afterthought, Spence had noted, "Some top Chinese leaders, who are masters at diplomatic nuances, have learned to take this approach when dealing with Westerners. It's both refreshing and surprising at the same time."

David listened while one of the representatives gave a long lecture on the American political system of representation and why most citizens weren't interested in or inclined to be more actively involved. David forced himself not to smile at the irony of this argument, since Spence had coached him not to smile when he disagreed or it would appear to the camera that he was agreeing. Instead, he simply looked pleasant but uncommitted.

Yes, representation is one of the keys to American success, David found himself debating in his mind with the speaker. *But so is local participation. Both are necessary, and either can be taken too far. In our modern world, the loss of local involvement has been a disaster.*

"My time has expired," the representative finally said.

"As everyone else has completed their five minutes," Chairperson Gibson said, "I will now take my allotted time."

Spence had warned David that Representative Gibson would be his most difficult challenge.

She turned to David: "Why do you hate the American system?" she asked bluntly.

"I don't," David countered amiably. "The genius of the American system is that each group has a say, that separate branches at all levels of government allow everyone to be involved in governance, and that checks and balances keep any one entity from having too much power.

"The challenge is that in recent decades, a lower percentage of the people are actively involved in our government. This development is a systemic challenge to democracy, and the Nine Resolves are designed precisely to overcome this problem. Moreover, we have so many excellent leaders in businesses and other fields around the nation that leaving their expertise and wisdom mostly out of governing our nation is a monumental waste of a huge national resource—"

Representative Gibson frowned and interrupted: "Are you a Republican or a Democrat? Do these Nine Resolves promote a conservative or a liberal agenda, in your mind?"

David smiled widely. "I'm not here to promote Republican or Democratic issues. I just want to see serious American improvement. We have so much leadership skill spread through the business leaders in our nation, and we are not tapping into it. It's time to unleash our great national resource of business leadership and truly begin fixing our biggest problems—"

"Are you trying to convince us that the gold standard is somehow democratic?" the chairwoman snapped.

"Actually, it is. When inflation comes, the wealthy aren't hurt because—"

She interrupted again. "How is the leading superpower in the world supposed to compete with China when we drastically reduce our tax revenues?"

Spence had prepared David well for this question. "The secret of the Chinese economy is consistent business growth, which actually brings increased tax revenues, and the best way to compete is to drastically incentivize similar or higher levels of growth in our own—"

"Have you ever held elected office? My notes say that you haven't. If you want to change things, why don't you let the voters decide?"

David remained unflustered. "Exactly my point. The entire

purpose of this hearing is to take the Nine Resolves to the voters so *they* can choose the future they—"

"How do you know your amendment will work?"

"The township system has been successfully tried repeatedly in American history. In fact, it was the basis of all thirteen colonies before the Constitutional Convention, and the Framers—"

"I find your answers unconvincing." Chairperson Gibson clipped him once again. "If you are going to come to a congressional hearing, you should come prepared. Especially if you are proposing an amendment to the Constitution itself—"

"I have an answer for each of your questions, but you haven't let me finish any of them. If you are going to ask questions, please give me the time to answer," David said with a bit of rising frustration.

Chairperson Gibson smiled.

Spence whispered into David's ear, "That's the clip everyone will see on TV tonight—you irritated in front of Congress."

Then in the microphone, Spence asked with a calm smile, "May we request a short break, Madame Chair?"

"Of course," Chairperson Gibson said smoothly. She had what she wanted, and she was only too happy to move on.

35

"Mr. Josh, sir. I'm enjoying being in this group, but I have a question."

"What is it?" Josh asked.

"Well, I've been wondering. Time is so fluid for us here...we have access to everything in the present and past, and we can fast-forward or rewind our screens back and forth however we want. But why can't we access the future?"

Sorry," David told the small group in the conference room. "It was just so annoying. She didn't let me finish a sentence. She kept peppering me with unrelated questions..."

"You're doing great," Amy assured him.

"No, you're not," Spence countered. "You answered the questions directly, which was good, but you let her get to you. To win this game, you have to—"

"Game!" David interrupted him. "Game? This isn't a game. This is the future of our nation. That's the whole problem. She is treating this whole thing like it's some sort of game. She wants to *win*. But this is bigger than winning and losing some political battle. What about the nation? What about the future of freedom?"

"Just like we practiced," Kami said quietly. "Look, she knows it's not a game. But she disagrees with you, and her tactics are working. If a lot of people watch C-SPAN, they'll see what she's doing.

But most Americans won't even hear about this, and those who do will see a ten-second sound bite of you acting annoyed. But it's not too late. We just need to get a different sound bite on tape."

"I agree," exclaimed Spence. "What's our strategy to replace what just happened with a sound bite that will work in our favor?"

David couldn't believe what he was hearing. He knew these people, and he knew how much they cared about freedom. But why were they so invested in the...*game? This is a serious and momentous occasion*, David thought. *Why are they treating the whole thing so, well, childishly?*

"May I offer a suggestion?"

The group turned at the voice, and the small red-haired man smiled nervously.

"How did you get past security?" Spence demanded.

"It's okay," Monte said. "This is our friend James, the one we told you about from San Diego."

"Oh," Spence said skeptically.

"You are always sneaking in and surprising us," David said. In reality, David was glad for the interruption. "How do you do that?"

"I'm small," James said, "and I guess I'm the quiet type. People just don't seem to notice me until I speak loudly. In any case, I watched your performance in the hearing, and I have a suggestion."

"Who are you, anyway...?" David started to say.

James hurried on: "The problem is that what you just did was exactly that, a performance. You were coached, trained, and prepared. You practiced for this, then went in with a list of dos and don'ts, as though you were following a script. Your answers are good, but you are playing a role, and the chairwoman is responding by playing her own role."

Everyone looked at James with rapt attention, and Kami slowly nodded.

"You are new to politics, and you want to do well, so you are trying to play this game the way the politicians do." James paused.

"Forgive me for calling it a game. I heard you earlier, and you are right—this isn't a game at all. But it appears that you are trying to fit in, *instead of leading*."

James let that idea settle with the group. Then he said, "What if the people really are the first branch of government? And what if you are just one of the people—no official title or position, just a concerned citizen trying to save freedom? If so, then these representatives work for you. With all due respect to them, you are their leader."

He could see that this fresh approach was sinking in.

"I don't mean to suggest that you should act smugly or lecture them about working for the people. They've heard it before, and it's a little clichéd. But you've led thousands of people for nearly all of your adult life. You've made a career of it.

"So as the leader you are, if you were in a hearing with all the top leaders you've worked with over the years, how would you approach them?"

The whole group was listening closely now. Wendell was taking notes, and even Spence nodded reluctantly.

"If you lose this vote," James continued, "that's the fault of the representatives. Most of them have already made up their minds, anyway. That's why it actually *is* a game, sort of, because their decisions were already made in discussions with supporters and top staff and party colleagues. The rest is for show, or at least most of it is.

"And the chairwoman is just responding to your energy and using your sincerity against you. She's had long practice at this, learned in the courtroom and from many years in political office. But she's not a bad person. Problem is, you haven't done anything to show her this isn't a game."

Nobody said anything, so James continued. "People buy into a leader first, and only then into the leader's vision. Have you heard this concept before?"

James ignored the looks of surprise and kept talking. "So you have a choice. You can go for credibility, or you can go for leadership. You can't do both. Nobody ever really does. One is always pilot and the other is copilot." James shuddered a little when he mentioned flying, but nobody noticed.

"You can try to fit in and to impress, or you can lead. And in leading, you have to say what needs to be said, and you let the chips fall wherever they fall. But in this town, in this building, in this environment, where almost everybody is trying to fit in and impress, the leader who truly leads is rare."

James paused. "Some of your modern books are so strange," he added whimsically. "For example, the novelist Ayn Rand lamented that her life hadn't been all it could have been because she wanted so badly to be highly acclaimed by the experts, especially the academic elite of her time. It wasn't enough to be brilliant—she felt a desperate desire to be acclaimed by those with prestige.

"Sadly for her, such recognition came only after she passed on, but imagine what she might have done if she had chosen leadership rather than trying to seek credibility. How many others have limited their impact on society for the same reason?

"In contrast, think of Lincoln, Churchill, and Gandhi—these are men who made the hard choice. They rejected trying to impress and instead they led. Not two in a thousand people will make this choice. Almost everyone, as John Adams said, seeks to impress others."

James slowed his speaking, and deliberately looked around the room. Then his eyes settled on David and he spoke slightly louder.

"But a few people do make a different choice. They take the lonely path of leadership, like the tall, old tree high above the timberline. They are often misunderstood, criticized, opposed. Their mistakes are part of public gossip, but their successes are often envied and always second-guessed. What they start, others come along and manage—but the managers would have nothing to do if the innovators hadn't led out.

"The managers talk about how the innovators made mistakes,

and how they, the managers, had to fix them. But without the innovators, there would be no big changes, no significant progress, no real greatness.

"Without them, there is no leadership, and ultimately no prosperity or freedom.

"So choose, David. Either go back in that room and try to fit in and impress people... or take the other path: walk in there and *lead*.

James paused, and the whole room waited breathlessly for his next words.

"But know this—millions will either suffer or benefit from your choice. That's the highest level of leadership. That's the LeaderShift you've been promoting to the nation."

Everyone watched him in stunned silence.

Finally, James spoke again. "Leading may not win you votes, but it will win you sound bites, and the sound bites will be watched by millions of Americans everywhere.

"Isn't that what this is all about?" he asked quietly. "If the future depends on elected officials, we've lost. Of course, our representatives play a vital role, but they are ultimately only a reflection of the people they represent. If you convince these officials but you don't reach the people, nothing will change—not really..."

He let his voice trail off. The whole room simply stared at him in awe.

James continued softly, "This isn't childish. It's real. And the regular people who make up this great nation, and other great nations in need of freedom, they are real, too. What you decide here *matters*. Freedom *matters*."

James sighed, and then he smiled. "Don't try to be credible, or to impress, or to fit in. Forget all your coaching, though it was clearly excellent. But forget it anyway. Don't play the game. Just lead."

He turned and headed toward the door, but David immediately stood and whispered, "Wait!"

He hadn't meant to whisper, but it came out that way after the emotion caused by James's words. "Please don't leave yet. I have a question," David said.

James turned and waited.

"I'm not sure how to phrase this...but, exactly, how do I lead? What does leading mean in this context? In this place?"

James smiled. "How would I know?" he asked softly. "I'm following *you* in all this. I'm amazed at what you've accomplished. I'm excited to see what you'll do next. You're the leader in this, so all I can tell you is this—go lead."

David nodded his head slowly.

"David," James repeated firmly, "your leadership has been outstanding so far. So, keep on leading."

This time nobody said anything as James left the room.

After a few moments, they all turned and looked at David.

David didn't notice, because he was staring at his hands. The room stayed silent for what seemed like a long time, then David looked up. His piercing eyes connected with everyone in the room, and Spence gasped quietly at the feeling that swept the room.

David said, "Thank you all for your incredible support. You are the best friends in the world." Then he stood. "It's time," he said.

The bell chimed, calling everyone back to the hearing. Kami would later recount with crisp clarity that David was already striding purposefully out the door when the chime rang.

Associated Press (Washington, D.C.)—When the Nine Resolves Amendment failed by one vote in the Senate eleven years ago, the resurgence of localism, more involvement of business leaders in government, and the idea that regular citizens are the first branch of government appeared to have ended with its defeat.

But after the global economic downturn and the Second Great Depression, the Ten Percent Party revitalized the economy as business leaders and other citizens rallied behind the principles of free enterprise, local townships, and unprecedented levels of citizen participation in governance.

The Ten Percent Party (not an official political party) was instrumental in increasing the power of the states and the creation of township-level governments around the nation. Business leaders in all fifty states used their influence in unprecedented levels to lead local community solutions for major problems.

Today another milestone was reached by the Ten Percent Party of business leaders when Florida, Utah, and Michigan became the last needed states to ratify the new Local Leadership Amendment. The proposal that brought this change was originally introduced in Congress four years ago by Senator Kami Stone (I-CA).

David Mersher, former CEO of Indytech and one of the longtime leaders of the Ten Percent movement, said, "This couldn't have happened without the voluntary leadership of thousands of regular citizens across the nation, including many leaders from business, industry, religious and family groups, and professionals from many arenas. The one common thread that unites them all is that they are regular American citizens who are deeply committed to ongoing participation in government."

Mersher was offered the position of Ambassador to the European Union when he retired from Indytech two years ago, but he declined, saying, "My role as a regular citizen is too important. I just don't have time to be an Ambassador and also keep a close enough eye on everyday government."

Critics of the Amendment, including Senator Cecil Huntington (R-MA), say that it is a blow to democracy (continued on A3)...

Epilogue

"I'm going to change the focus of Group 1, sir."

"Why? What do you have in mind?"

"Well, to tell the truth, I'm not entirely sure yet. I have an idea, but...it's complicated. Group 2 is making significant progress simulating what would have happened if we had officially added the local system at the Constitutional Convention. It's not all pretty. The changes in the status of women and people of all races have made the local thing much more effective in David's time than in 1787."

"That makes sense. So what about Group 1?"

"Well, actually, I want to redirect Group 2's focus to something David said about the Anti-Federalists being right on a lot of things. What if we had listened? We were so focused on ratification, we may have missed the opportunity to improve our system. I'll let you know what they find."

"Okay, that's Group 2. But what about Group 1? You seem to be avoiding this question."

James laughed. "Yes, sir. I guess you're right. I'm not sure what you're going to think about this."

The tall man sat down and took off his spectacles. "Okay, James, just tell me."

"Yes, sir. Well, it was a big transition to wonder what things we could have done better. My focus had been on how to help those in

the present day get things right, and I didn't notice what was right under my eyes."

"What is that?"

"Well, sir, the reality that if I can go down in the present and the past, I can go down in my own time, too. As a simulation, of course."

"You know that if you go down as yourself—in real life rather than simulation—you'll ruin everything. A few have tried, and it always ends badly."

"Yes, sir, I know. That's why I'll only do it in simulations on the big viewing screens."

The man gave James a knowing look. "James, I know you don't care about fitting in or impressing. You're an innovator, a founder, a pioneer. You push the limits, because that's how you are built. So, tell me what you're really planning."

"I promise, sir, I'm not going to go down to my own time."

"Yes, you said that. But what exactly are you going to do?"

James hesitated, but he realized his mentor wasn't going to relent. "Okay," he said, "I'm going to do something unprecedented: I'm going to send David to 1787..."

Do You Want to Be Part of the 10 Percent?

Visit TenPercentLeaderShift.com

About the Authors

ORRIN WOODWARD is the coauthor of the *New York Times* best-seller *Launching a Leadership Revolution*. In addition, Orrin's first solo book, *RESOLVED: 13 Resolutions for LIFE*, is listed in the Top 100 All-Time Best Leadership Books and he was awarded the 2011 Independent Association of Business (IAB) Leader of the Year Award. Orrin cofounded two multimillion-dollar leadership companies and is the chairman of the board of LIFE Business. He has a BS from GMI-EMI (now Kettering University) in manufacturing systems engineering. He holds four U.S. patents, and won an exclusive National Technical Benchmarking Award. He follows the sun between residences in Michigan and Florida with his lovely wife, Laurie, and their children. Orrin's leadership thoughts are shared on his blog: orrinwoodwardblog.com.

Born and raised in the American Southwest, OLIVER DEMILLE collects rocks, knives, watches, old books, and sunsets. His quest for a Founders-like education has defined his life and mission, and led to the founding of The Center for Social Leadership and an educational movement for our time known as Thomas Jefferson Education (TJEd). He is a popular keynote speaker, a sought-after mentor, and a two-time recipient of the Gold Honor Medal from the Freedoms Foundation at Valley Forge. Oliver is the author or coauthor of *Leadership Education*, *A Thomas Jefferson Education*, *The Student Whisperer*, *The Coming Aristocracy*, *The Four Lost American Ideals*, *1913*, and *FreedomShift*—among others. Oliver and his wife, Rachel, are raising their eight children in Cedar City, Utah. Subscribe to his blog at OliverDeMille.com.

**BUSINESS
PLUS**

Recognized as one of the world's most prestigious business imprints, Business Plus specializes in publishing books that are on the cutting edge. Like you, to be successful we always strive to be ahead of the curve.

Business Plus titles encompass a wide range of books and interests—including important business management works, state-of-the-art personal financial advice, noteworthy narrative accounts, the latest in sales and marketing advice, individualized career guidance, and autobiographies of the key business leaders of our time.

Our philosophy is that business is truly global in every way, and that today's business reader is looking for books that are both entertaining and educational. To find out more about what we're publishing, please check out the Business Plus blog at:

www.bizplusbooks.com